Trickle–Down Memory

Trickle-Down Memory

Susan Gregory

Order this book online at www.trafford.com
or email orders@trafford.com

Most Trafford titles are also available at major online book retailers.

Printed in the United States of America.

ISBN: 978-1-4269-5677-5 (sc)
ISBN: 978-1-4269-5678-2 (hc)
ISBN: 978-1-4269-5679-9 (e)

Library of Congress Control Number: 2011902480

Trafford rev. 06/28/2011

 www.trafford.com

North America & international
toll-free: 1 888 232 4444 (USA & Canada)
phone: 250 383 6864 ♦ fax: 812 355 4082

First Term

1956 - 1960

Trickle Down Memories

This is the story of one missionary family and the work that God did around and through them. My husband, George Harris Gregory (Harris) had a vision of doing things for the Lord with the talents the Lord had endowed him with. My job was to keep up with him and fit in with his plans wherever the Lord led us. Our children, to whom this book is dedicated, Chris, Melody, Mark, Becky and Lance, were on the sidelines looking on.

I want to thank Gloria Altenbernt and the members of the Writers Club here in Bradenton Missionary Village who inspired me and gave correction. I also want to thank the Arnett family, especially Crystal, who helped me with the typing. Last but not least is my mother-in-law, Lillian Parent Gregory. To her I give special homage as she stashed away our letters through the years. My memories would be very sketchy without those letters that told of our day to day lives.

I got the title "Trickle Down Memories" in the middle of a sleepless night. I was thinking about Harris and our lives together, after he'd gone to be with the Lord in 2006. I wanted those memories to trickle down, not only to our children, but our grandchildren and their children and who knows who else. This is our legacy to all of them. I hope our spiritual children will profit from it and know what a joy it was to lead them to our Savior. So join us in our trip down memory lane. I hope it will become a part of your heritage too.

A song that kept running through my mind was "Cannels Only" by Mary E. Maxwell. It's not what we do that counts but what the Lord does through us. We are channels.

How I praise thee, precious Savior
That thy love laid hold of me.
Thou hast saved and cleansed
and filled me
That I might thy channel be.

Channels only, blessed Master-
But with all thy wondrous power
Flowing thru us, Thou canst use
us
Every day and every hour.

Wouldn't it be wonderful if the Lord would come soon and we could all be together in heaven? Maybe God is waiting so that you will be there too. Someone has said, "Separation is the law of earth, but Reunion is the law of heaven." We'll all be one united family there. I'm looking forward to our big reunion in heaven. Becky and her family worked two years on an album for our 50th Wedding Anniversary. They also treated all of the family to a banquet at Homers. Then the rest of our children joined them in honoring us with a surprise evening of celebration with friends and neighbors at Shepherd Christian Community in Frostproof. It was special; a reunion and all being together again. It's impossible to imagine what it will be like when we all get to heaven. What a day of rejoicing that will be!

We Remember Papa

We Remember 'Papa – Our Tribute', by Susan Briggs Gregory Read at the funeral of Lester Briggs (May 12, 1898 – March 15, 1992).

Many of you here today only knew Lester Briggs as an old man – stooped, almost blind, and hard of hearing. He was almost 94 years old and able to keep on going because of the faithfulness of his two daughters, Janet and Mina, and occasional help from Willard, his son.

Few know of his background and consistent faithfulness to his family and fervent love for the Lord. This has been such a great heritage for his daughters, sons and grandchildren.

Dad came from a big family. He had seven brothers and two sisters who grew up in the Briggs homestead in Kewanee, Illinois. Walter Briggs, his father, died when he was in his fifties—killed when he was struck by a car. The whole family learned to pull together and support their mother, Mina Briggs.

In 1918 Dad met Mary Mulholland, a pretty young school teacher. He married her in 1921. For most of his life he worked as a railway mail clerk – sorting mail as the trains rolled. It was a steady job even during the depression. At first they lived in the Chicago area but there was much illness in the family. So in 1933 they moved back to Kewanee. He commuted the 130 miles to Chicago, so that his children could be raised on familiar territory near friends and relatives.

Almost every Sunday, Dad's brothers and sisters would gather at the Briggs homestead across the field from our house. We were brought up among many aunts and uncles, and cousins. Our mother's sister and brother and families also lived in the same town, as well as many other second and third cousins.

Dad and mother both had a real relationship with Jesus Christ and were desirous that their children be raised in a God-fearing, loving Christian home. Church, Bible readings and living based on Christian principles were basic pillars in our home. We weren't forced into it – it was just our life we entered into as a family. We praise the Lord for this heritage. It worked. All their children came to know the Lord as their Savior and went on to live for him.

As we three older ones were growing up dad and mom started a 'second family': first Mina and then two years later Ronnie. Ronnie was a hemophiliac and was only with us four years. In those days little was known about hemophilia and our family united in meeting his special needs and crisis. We all learned much from Ronnie. Sue especially profited from their love and attitude toward him, as the Lord later entrusted her husband and her with a special hemophilic son for 18 years.

As we grew up and left home, our parents were always there when needed and to encourage us. Janet went to Bolivia as a missionary, eventually Sue and her family to Brazil. Our parents were among our most enthusiastic supporters in prayer and financially. As the Lord provided they gave liberally, often sacrificially that their children could share God's word with others.

They always were active and faithful in serving the Lord themselves. They were active in their own church as well as Child Evangelism classes, teaching at Home Missions, and helping those in need or ill. Dad also served on the board of D&D Missionary Homes. There he also took his work seriously. He helped reroofing houses, painting, repairing anything that needed to be done, so that missionaries would have a place to stay while on furlough or ill. Hundreds of missionaries have been able to profit from this including Sue's family who spent a total of three years there on furloughs.

As we gather today: children, grandchildren and friends, each one has their own memories of how he met their needs – a down payment on a house, a car, a word of correction, a word of encouragement.

Now Dad has been reunited with Mom and they're with the Lord they both loved and taught us to love. We're sure he heard the Lord say, "Well done, good and faithful servant. Enter into the things which I have prepared for you."

We'll all miss Dad. But his life and example will always be with us. We look forward to the time when we will join them around God's throne. The patriarch of our family will be standing tall – his mission in life accomplished. Will his 15 grandchildren, 27 great-grandchildren, and two great—great-grandchildren be there too? Dad did his part. Now we are to 'carry on the torch' and continue serving the Lord as he did.

Our Stories

Deuteronomy 4:9 ~ Only take heed to yourself and diligently keep yourself lest you forget the things your eyes have seen, and lest they depart from your heart all the days of your life: and teach them to your children and your grandchildren.

Life's truest heroes never carve their names
On marble columns built for their acclaim.
They build instead a legacy that springs
From faithful service to their King of Kings.
~Gustafson

I have an unusual opportunity of leaving a message for present and future generations – a unique story. A legacy of lives lived for God. My story starts with Christian parents bringing up their children in the fear and admonition of the Lord. I was saved at an early age and was fascinated by missionaries and their experiences since early days. My sister, Janet Briggs, who was 6 years older than me, went to Bolivia as a missionary while I was in my teens.

Harris and his brother Eugene (fourteen months younger) attended the Gregory family church but never understood the plan of salvation, even though their parents were Christians. Their parents, George H. Gregory Sr. and Lillian M. became concerned about their sons leaving home without Christ, and began attending First Baptist church of Asbury Park in Harris' senior year of high school. During that year, he came under conviction and accepted Christ as his Savior.

His father's family owned a florist business. To prepare to be a part of that, he had a scholarship to Rutgers University. After he was saved, his parents decided he should attend a Christian college for at least one year. He enrolled at Bob Jones College in Cleveland, TN. During a Bible Conference his first year there, he wrote home to his folks that he was thinking very seriously of going into mission work. "I am just going to let the Lord lead and everything will work perfectly," he wrote.

Harris' maternal grandmother had died just before his mother was married. She had a brother a lot younger than herself, who she helped raise, and he spent a lot of time at their house because of his mother's death. As Harris grew up, he followed his uncle Vic around helping him in his activities: working on cars, motorcycles, boats, and anything that needed fixing around the house. Harris became very adept at fixing things while watching his uncle. In his second year at Bob Jones College, Harris decided to follow this experience, and transferred to John Brown University the next year so that he could major in engineering.

While at Bob Jones, we had become engaged, so I also went to John Brown University the next year. We were married in 1948. In 1949, he graduated with a major in aeronautical engineering and a minor in mechanical engineering. Harris had also gotten his pilots license and A&E mechanics license for working on airplanes.

After graduation, we went back to New Jersey, but Harris had lost interest in the florist business. He got a job in construction until a position in engineering opened up at Fort Monmouth, N.J. There he worked as a civilian employee in research and development with the United States Government. He traveled quite a bit, going to military bases all over the U.S., to accomplish his work. He was cleared for top level security for this, and loved his job. We built our own home on land his grandparents had given us. To all appearances, missionary work had been forgotten.

We were active in the church were Harris had been saved. We also helped another couple in planting another church, Collingswood Baptist Church, working with young people's groups. We also started a group called 'Co-Pilots' at Asbury Park Baptist for young married couples that created much interest among couples with young children. By that time Harris and I had three children.

In 1956, when the five missionaries were killed in Ecuador, Harris and I both felt the Lord had more for us than this. We applied to South America Indian Mission and went to their candidate class in May of 1956. In August of the same year, we were on our way by ocean liner to Brazil with our three children: (Chris (7), Melody (3), and Mark (1).

Besides our parents and personal friends, we were supported by the church in Asbury Park and Bethany Presbyterian Church in Fort Lauderdale, Florida. These two churches continued to support our ministry the entire time we were in missions. Later, The Baptist Tabernacle in Belmar, New Jersey; Avon Park Baptist in Avon By the Sea, New Jersey; Laurelton Park Baptist in Brick, New Jersey; Northside Baptist Church in St. Petersburg, FL, and Faith Community Church in Pensauken, New Jersey supported our ministry. What a blessing it was to have faithful supporters encouraging us.

The Gregory's Leave for Brazil

"A large group of friends of Mr. and Mrs. Harris Gregory, Sea Girt, NJ went by bus to New York to bid farewell to the Gregory family who sailed yesterday for Brazil on the Moore McCormick Argentina where they will serve as missionaries. Mr. and Mrs. Gregory were accompanied by their three children: Chris, Melody, and Mark. they will serve as missionaries in the jungles of Brazil among the Indians never before contacted by white men. They plan to stay in the jungles for five years under the sponsorship of the interdenominational South America Indian Mission."

-Asbury Park Press, August 31, 1956

11

Highlights from our seventeen day boat trip.

"The weather has been nice. We had a couple of short showers yesterday. We haven't seen land, a boat, or anything but water for three days. The children have been very good. They have plenty of playmates. There are 89 children in cabin class and 175 in first class. Also in cabin class there are 39 missionaries. Several are going to Campinas for language study, and several are veteran missionaries. It's very interesting to find out their different stories. We've been getting around a piano and singing at night. We have a Bible study too. Harris has been learning Portuguese from an agriculturist. Chris plays with a girl, who is Brazilian but knows English too, and he has picked up a lot of words from her."

"The food is wonderful. I'm glad we didn't bring our bathroom scales. The waiter always has a surprise for the children – fancy food, a little toy, or balloons. They have a nursery on the boat, but we don't leave them there too often as there are so many children. They do enjoy going there, though. We walked up to first class deck the other night. When we got back Chris said, "Whee! At last we're back in our own class. I feel better here. This is much nicer." Guess we just aren't raising first class kids.

We've only gone swimming a couple of times. The pools are all 5 and a half feet deep. Chris and Melody soon got cold, but Mark loved it and stayed in a long time. I think he'd jump in the ocean if we would let him.

We'll be in Trinidad tomorrow, and Barbados the next day. At Trinidad, the boat docked way out and we had an hour ride by motor launch. That was a new experience for us all.

Our day in Barbados was an interesting experience. We had a ten minute ride by motor launch to reach land. Before our boat even stopped moving, the water was swarming with native divers waiting to dive for your nickels, dimes, and quarters. The business district was also very interesting. People were pulling all different kinds of carts themselves, and a lot more were balancing their wares on their heads. Our baby carriage was quite an oddity to them with our blonde children. At one time we had 30 or 40 natives gaping over Mark, who was asleep. One woman wanted to trade a little black boy for him. In the afternoon we went swimming. Harris especially enjoyed that swim in the crystal clear water.

Tuesday, the 13th, they surprised us with a birthday cake for Melody. It was a delicious cake with several layers, different fillings, and very fancy decorations. That's the best birthday cake she has ever had. Joe, the waiter, gave her a jar of candy he had gotten in Barbados. She carried the candy around for days, and wrapped it and unwrapped it dozens of times. So far, they've only eaten two candies (by now it has joint ownership – Chris has taken over). They are saving the rest for Christmas, they say. Several of the other missionaries have remarked on how unusually good our waiter is. He goes up to first class and brings us back special things. He says that he enjoys doing things for people who appreciate it. So we're trying to show him that we rally do appreciate it.

The captain's party was last night, and it was quite an affair. The children loved it. Everybody was throwing spaghetti, sauce, and dead fish all over. King Neptune boarded the boat at the equator. Right now we have 24 balloons in our room. To eat, we had our choice of lobster, filet mignon, or baby turkey. We got turkey for Mark, and the rest of us got the filet mignon. Of course, Harris had two, or was it three?

We saw our first bare kids in Sao Salvador Baia, Brazil. It was quite a day. We went with three other missionaries, and the couple's two small daughters. The fellow of the couple is the son of missionaries, and he had lived in Brazil and knew Portuguese. Baia is on two levels. The markets are on the lower level, and then you take a big elevator, winding roads, or cable car to the upper, or more modern, level. Our biggest problem was the carriage. You couldn't go on cable cars, street cars, or buses with it. They almost weren't going to let us go on the elevator. So finally we took a taxi. In Rio, we're going to take the carriage one day, and just visit shops. The other day, we'll just ride around and see sights. They have a zoo, and also an amusement park, so Chris is excited about that.

When we docked in Rio at noon on Thursday, we expected to be alone in the big city. Rio is something – mountains all around made for quite a view from the ocean liner. I was finishing getting the kids ready to go ashore when we docked, but Harris was out on the deck. He was really surprised when someone called his name from down below. The field director, Ernie Lubkeman, had come down to Rio, and had recognized Harris from the picture in the Amazon Valley Mission magazine. Ernie and the MAF pilot, Jim Lomheim, who was to be in our area, were there. Jim had to take an examination in the afternoon so that he could pilot a plane in Brazil.

Ernie took us to the Indian Protection Service Museum. It had all kinds of displays on Indians. Then he showed us around Rio. Chris got his hoped for ride on the bonde (open street car). We also took the cable car ride up to the top of Sugar Loaf Mountain. We were up there when all the lights of Rio came on. It was really pretty. We almost missed supper, but just made the deadline with Ernie and Jim as our guests. They really enjoyed the meal, getting things to eat that they hadn't eaten for a long time. After dinner we put our kids to bed, as they were really tired from their day in Rio. We went out for awhile to see Rio's night-life. Then we saw Jim off on the bus to Campinas where he and his wife are in language study.

Friday we saw more of Rio with Ernie. We went up to the Cristo Redemptor. It's a big statue of Christ on top of a mountain overlooking Rio. What a ride it was to get there, and another amazing view of Rio. Then Ernie came back and had lunch with us on the boat. While the kids took their nap in the afternoon, we saw more of the city. Ernie took the bus from Rio at 4 p.m., so as to meet our boat in Santos. Our boat sailed at 6 p.m. We were thankful we had someone to take us around Rio who knew the city and the language.

They woke us up at 6 a.m. to tell us to go up and clear with the immigration officials, as we were getting off the boat in Santos. That was the beginning of a hectic day, but it was wonderful how the Lord worked it all out for us. Another big boat from England had docked the same time that we had. There was a pile of people to go through customs. It's a big place, but it was packed. Waiting was the hardest part for the children.

Finally, our number was called at about 1 p.m. We went in and got all our luggage together, unlocked, and opened; waiting for the inspector to go through them. They let Ernie go in with us. Ernie had hired a customs man to help us, and the customs man explained to the inspector that we were missionaries with just personal effects. The customs man had even gone into the pile of papers and pulled ours out from way down in the pile. They were really easy on us. Praise the Lord. Some of the inspectors were really ripping things apart. Another missionary had two huge wooden boxes, and had to take everything out of them. Our inspector just lifted a few corners and hardly messed anything up. He didn't even look in the barrels at all. He took the lid off of one and asked what was in them. We gave him our itemized list, and he was satisfied with that. He charged us $35 for the accordion, $20 for the radio, and $15 for all the rest. Ernie had arranged for a truck to take it all to the railroad station, which cost another $70. Then we took a taxi from Santos to Sao Paulo. Ernie went on the truck with the baggage.

The next day, we went to the American consulate and registered. We got our checks cashed, exchanged into Brazilian currency, and opened a bank account. Then we went to a snake farm, Bom Tao Tao, where most of the remedies for snake bites come from. A lot of very dangerous snakes are there, as well as spiders and other poisonous things.

Ernie has been telling us about our house in Aquidauana. It sounds nice. They're giving us one of their maids. He says that she is clean, really nice, knows some English, eighteen, and wonderful with children. Her name is Ruthie.

Chacara Aguazul/Aquidauana

Harris always liked westerns and that kind of life. He'll have it in Aquidauana, Matto Grosso, Brazil. I'll let him tell about it.

"Aquidauana is like a wild/west town. There are more horses than trucks or jeeps and no cars. The taxis are two wheel horse drawn carts. There are ox carts too pulling heavy loads. The streets are pretty empty most of the time except for people walking. All the streets are dirt except in the center of town. They started paving there three months ago with cements blocks one foot square and four inches thick.

"We have ordered our furniture to be made. The carpenter shop is like a small lumber mill. All our furniture is of clear cedar, solid and beautifully made. We ordered one double bed, two chest of drawers, two night tables, one large chifferobe with three doors and three drawers (there are no closets in the house), two large square tables, six dining room chairs with upholstered seats, and one large buffet. Otherwise, any furnishings are footlockers, barrels, or boards. The children will sleep on the cots we brought and Mark has his netted crib.

"Our home is still being painted. We hope to be in it sometime in October. It has four huge rooms with an outside patio in back. The bathroom and maids quarters are off of that on one side and the kitchen on the other side. The kitchen is crude with a wood burning stove, deep cemented sink (for washing dishes and clothes), and a table. All the windows have wooden shutters without glass or screens. It is all kind of

16

barn-like with no ceilings. The double front door locks like a barn door with a wooden bar across on the inside.

Until our house is finished we are staying at Chacara Aguazul. The Bible Institute is here with dormitory students. There are three resident missionary families here and a single girl and fellow. He, Geddy Strickland, had polio and is still in language study. He will live in a small house behind ours and share our bathroom. Also one of the missionary wives Ruth Harmon, had polio a couple of years ago, leaving one of her legs completely paralyzed and the other not too good. You really have to give her credit. She accomplishes so much even though she has braces on both legs and is in a wheel chair. She and her husband Charles "Chuck" Harmon have have two young children here and two in the states studying. The Field Director, Ernie Lubkeman lives here with his wife leona, two boys a little older than Chris and a girl Melody's age. Husband Bud McArthur and his family are the third couple. His wife Regina is a nurse. All of the adults teach at the Bible Institute.

Sunday, we had quite a ride and really felt like missionaries. We went with Ruth Harmon to hold a meeting at a Terena Indians home. We went in the Harmon's jeep. It took an hour to go and a half hour to come back. Harris, known as Senhor Jorge here, drove and got his first taste of driving on these "lovely" roads. It took him awhile to become accustomed to them. It was a struggle just to stay in our seats, but somehow Mark slept all the way home. I don't know how.

Of course the children love it here with plenty of playmates. Chris rode a horse today, all by himself. They all want a horse now. I don't know if that is a good idea or not – three young children and a horse in the same yard. We do have a cement wall all around the two houses that goes up six feet with three rows of barbed wire on top of that. Mark even got a ride and sat right up on top of the horse by himself, proud as a peacock. All of us love the outdoor feeling here. Our Chris and Billy Lubkeman built a tree house one day while we were gone, which was Chris' lifelong ambition. The kids have practically lived in it ever since. We eat all of our meals outdoors in a covered area between the kitchen/living room part of the house and the bedrooms.

The insects and spiders haven't bothered us too much. We have seen some huge tarantulas. They throw alcohol on them and burn them up. It's the hairs on the tarantulas that cause skin irritation and burning. They do that with scorpions too. There are immense toads here that croak all night and when it rains. All of the bedrooms here have screens on the windows and covered walkways so that the rain and the vermin don't usually get in.

Baptismal Service in Bananal

It was decided that all the missionaries in language study should go to Taunai where the churches in the area of Ipague/Taunai/Bananal were having a baptismal service. Bob and Rita Wright (Jonathan – six months) and Ginny Viets, who had been in our candidate class, had recently arrived and we would be staying with the Winfred Buckman (Buck) family.

We left Aquidauana on the 10:30 AM train on Saturday and returned on the 3 PM train on Monday. The kids were thrilled to be riding on the wood burning steam engine train. There are no roads to Taunai, so everything is brought in by rail. Mark was so exhausted from all the excitement of getting ready that he went right to sleep and slept all the way there.

Buck and his children (Larry 11 and Susie 7) met us at the station. We made quite a sight lugging it all (children, suitcases, jungle hammocks, Mark's bed, everybody's bedding) the mile or so to the Buckman's house. We were fortunate to have a whole bedroom to ourselves. The Wrights had the living room, Ginny and a Brazilian girl had the schoolroom, the maids the kitchen, the Buckmans their bedroom. Geddy Strickland and Bud McArthur slept in the church. We had a single bed and a cot pushed together in our room. Crazy us, we thought we wouldn't bother with the jungle hammocks. So Chris slept at one end of the bed with Harris at the other, and I slept with Melody on the cot. What a night! The mosquitoes feasted on Melody all night even though the house was screened. The Buckmans hadn't lived there too long and there were spaces between the roof and the walls they didn't have screen on yet. The next night we put the kids in the jungle hammocks, which solved the problem for them. Even so, we fared better than some of the others.

The Wrights had never used their jungle hammocks and one of them was strung wrong. That was Rita's, every time she'd go to get in it she'd flip over two or three times. It was the first time that Jonathan had ever slept in a hammock and he kept waking up. Every time Rita got up to tend to him the hammock would start rolling again. By morning she was a nervous wreck and didn't care about sleeping in a jungle hammock ever again.

I said that Ginny slept in the school room. The first night the hammocks of both hers and the Brazilian girl, who was to be baptized the next day, kept breaking down. So finally Buck took them across the street to the school teacher's house to sleep, as she had a bed there they could use. All night Ginny said there were bats swooping and rats crawling. In those homes it is just like one big room and the lady was sleeping with four kids in one bed. All night long somebody was jumping out of bed to go on the potty beside the bed. The littlest girl had asthma bad and was real sick all night; you can imagine how much sleep Ginny had! But we had a real good time comparing experiences the next morning.

I forgot to tell you about the wedding we attended in the afternoon after we arrived. Two people were getting married so that they could be baptized the next day. They already had three children—a good start for any marriage ceremony. Francis had told Rita, Ginny and me to go on ahead as it was near to their home, and she would come later. When we got there, nobody knew what to do next. Somebody showed us to some seats. Come to find out later, it was the seats for the bride and groom; we had to vacate the premises. The wedding ceremony is civil – real important looking officials were there with their wives as witnesses. After they read all the facts from the record, they had all these people sign the record. All of a sudden the head man called me up to write my name down as a witness. I didn't even know the name of the people or anything about them, but I didn't want to attempt to explain all that to them in my faltering Portuguese, so I signed my name. Some witness! Harris had gone up to Bananal with Buck in the afternoon. He said they had four or five weddings up there of people who were getting married so that they would be able to be baptized.

Sunday was a busy day. We left the house at 8:30 and never got back until 5 PM. Because of the big baptismal service, all the churches in the area were having a combined service. It was at Bananal which is quite a ride from the church in Taunai, I do mean quite a ride in more ways than one. They had rented three big trucks for the day to take everyone from Taunai and other places. They were all packed. Of course the roads were awful and the guy who was driving was hurrying to pick up more. We had quite a time keeping our equilibrium. There were five or six hundred people there for the Baptismal Service, maybe more. After the service we walked a couple of miles to the tanks (it looked like a lake to me but guess the "tanques" had been dug out.) Bud and Buck baptized forty-four people, two at a time. Each one gave their testimony first so you can imagine that it took quite awhile. By that time Mark was really getting tired and was quite fussy, so I didn't get to see too much of the baptismal. But it was a thrill to know that results were being seen in this place after years of faithful work.

After that was over we hiked the two miles back to the school yard for dinner. They had a churasco (meat cooked over an open fire). The meat was a little tough but the kids thought it was wonderful and by then we were all ready to eat anything.

After lunch they had another service at the church. Then they also served communion for the first time to the ones who had just been baptized, as well as to all the believers. Buck is very easy for us to understand – he has very good Portuguese and speaks clear and slow – which is good for us. During this meeting, I had put Mark to sleep in a hammock, so I stayed outside with him. The outside was packed, as well as the inside. It was mostly women and children outside.

The ride up had been bad enough but the ride home was really awful. We had more people than ever on the truck and I was sitting down with both Mark and Melody on my lap. After awhile, Harris got in a position where he could take Melody. Somebody was always falling on us. My rear was actually black and blue the next day from the ride. But we really enjoyed the day in spite of being awfully tired and achy. We rejoiced with those who had taken this step forward in their Christian life. That night we went to the church service at the Taunai church.

Divided Household

After we had been in language study for a year Harris was asked to build a house for Dudley and Dotty Kinsman at a new station among the Nhambiquara Indians in the northwest corner of Mato Grosso. Meanwhile Susan and the children stayed on in Aquidauana in southern Mato Grosso. We'll have Susan's story first.

Language study continued and I also spent time translating all our flannel graph stories into Portuguese. On Sunday I taught the Sunday School class for teenage girls and a week day meeting with them where they sewed and did different projects. At this time they were making clothes for an orphanage in Jardim. I also cooperated with Ginny Viets and Rita Wright in children and women's meetings. These and the duties of the home and children and teaching Chris "Calvert's Course" was enough to keep me busy. Almost every week Ginny and I would go and have a meeting down in back of our house at an old Indian believer's house.

We usually went right after supper taking medications and band aids with us. This particular night we had been delayed by treating a badly infected foot of a little neighbor girl. By the time we got there for the meeting it was starting to get dark. The Lord had really been blessing at those meetings. The people never came out too much when we had the services there in the daytime, but since we'd started it after supper everybody over there came. Just Melody went over with Ginny and me that night. We started the meeting and by the time we got through singing it was quite dark. Somebody had made a small fire for light because they didn't have electricity there.

All of a sudden a young man went into a seizure. He had come to us for medicine several times and from what he told us I said to Ginny that I thought he was having epileptic seizures. He was sitting right near us holding a little girl – a year and a half old. He started howling and shaking all over. I had the accordion on so I couldn't get to the little girl and I thought for sure that he would fall over before anyone got her. Just as soon as somebody got her he went over on the ground and really had a severe seizure. I said to Ginny that here was another example of how the Lord prepares you in so many ways. Two young people in our church in New Jersey had seizures every so often. I had seen them and how the people took care of them and they were no danger to anyone else. He was practically on top of our feet so Ginny and I got behind our chairs and I put Melody behind hers too. I wasn't thinking too much about her reaction until she looked up at me and said, "Is he dying?", and "Why are we standing behind our chairs?" She was really expecting something to happen and it must have been quite scary for her. So I explained it was an illness and to pray for him. I guess I did all right, because she came home and told Chris all about it and there didn't seem to be any fear.

After the seizure he fell into a deep sleep. He made noises even while he was sleeping. But we just went on with the meeting. We sang while he quieted down some. Then I stood there beside him and told the story. That was under different circumstances than I've ever done it before. They say he just has the seizures when there is a full or new moon.

Building a New Station

Assignment for Harris Gregory to build a house for the Kinsmans' in the Alto Guapore:

Dudley Kinsman and a friend had gone to Sao Paulo to get Dudley's new truck out of customs. On the way back Dud left Olaf in Campo Grande with the two trucks and went on to Aquidauana on the train to get Harris. I'll quote from Harris' letters to tell about his first foray into jungle living.

"We left Camp Grande the first of February, 1958, and little did I know I wouldn't return until the middle of May. It took us six days to get to Cuiaba. Halfway there Dudley's older truck broke the transmission gears and the new truck had to pull it the rest of the way. The road was terrible with deep ruts and we got stuck a few times. The new truck had a winch though and ten tires and it went right through the mud and pulled the old one out onto solid ground.

"From Cuiaba I flew to a new Station with Jim Lomheim, the MAF pilot, where the Chavanti Indians are at the Botavi. These Indians were the ones that attacked our missionaries when they tried to make contact with them. They lived in the deep jungle and had never had a peaceful contact with civilization at that time. As I climbed out of the airplane I stood face to face with a naked Chavanti warrior armed with his bow and arrow. Over 300 of these Indians have moved to the government posts where our missionaries can live nearby and work with them. They are still very primitive, but about half of them wear some clothes. How helpless I felt not being able to talk to them. As yet, very little of their language is known, and not enough to bring the story of salvation to them. We visited another reservation at the Paranatinga where there were 100 more Chavanti Indians and about 200 Bacari and Iranche Indians.

"Wherever I go they have me fixing things. My reputation as a fixer has gotten around. In Cuiaba while the Kinsmans were doing their buying and loading the truck, I worked on the Halverson's car, a Model-A Ford. Mr. Halverson really appreciated it and said, "It's never worked this good.""

"From Cuiaba I continued on with the Kinsmans in their new truck. The new station is around 700 road miles northwest of Cuiaba. In a plane it's about 305 air miles and takes about 4 hours to fly the MAF plane. My mission was to build their house out of native materials. It was the rainy season and the rivers (the headwaters of the Amazon River) were the highest in years. All the bridges are crude and were covered with water, except one. The trip took over a week. Animals: deer, tapir and emu were plentiful so we had a lot of meat to eat.

"On a couple of the bridges we had to unload half of the load and carry everything across. The truck dipped hard once and the Indian helper fell off the truck. I was sitting right up front just over the cab (less branches there). I la n de don top of the cab and dented the roof, but it popped right out. An Indian woman and her children were in the middle of the load which was the safest place. On other dips the dog fell off and almost hung himself before we noticed him. Another time he fell off and the chain broke and it took an hour to find him.

"At the halfway point there was an abandoned house and a small clear stream. On their trip from the previous station they had left three Nhambiquara men to guard their possessions which were in a sealed room. We unloaded half of the truck and Dottie, their son Danny, and the Nhambiquara woman and her children remained there. Their plan was to leave me alone at the new station while Dud went back for the women and the second load.

"The next day, in spite of a tropical storm, we got past Rio Verde. We were on top of the Serra dos Parecis where the Parecis, a semi-civilized tribe live. Our next stop was the baracao (headquarters of rubber hunters) of a man called Kangaroo. The MAF plane arrived there at noon as planned. Dud had also left things there, so another reload took place. The rubber hunters are mainly rough criminals that have been released from prisons and allowed to go to that isolated area to take sap from the rubber trees. Just before we arrived, one man shot another in the head and we had to move the body to get to Dud's things.

"When we arrived at the location of the new SAM station there were no Indians except the ones that had come with us. We put them to work clearing the area where the Kinsman's house was to be built. It is in a beautiful location.

"We three went up in the plane to look for the Indians that should have arrived already. Later we searched by truck without success. The truck broke a part that held the oil filter and we had to abandon it an hours walk away. This will delay going back for the women and children. A trip up here by plane costs around $125.00 so that makes broken parts expensive and time consuming. In my spare time until the Indians arrived, I surveyed the area for a place we could build. I also named two capiseiras after Suzanne and Melodia. These are two small rivers originating in this area. Finally 45 Indians arrived to help in the cutting and splitting of the palm trees.

LATER

"The work is progressing and all of the Kinsman family are here now with their belongings. The house has a hanger for the plane that also serves for meetings with the Indians, and a place for them to eat. Dottie is kept busy supervising the women in the food preparation for all of us.

"The food is kept in metal barrels with locks on them: brown sugar cakes (rapadura), beans, rice, flour and ground corn. The first trip they had brought some Indians and they planted yucca (a big root they use to make their Indian bread. It can also be used like potatoes. That's pretty much the Indian diet while they are here. They can really eat. Occasionally they do gown into the deep jungle and kill ant eaters, wild pigs, tapir, monkeys, and other small animals. They eat them right there as climbing back up isn't conducive to bringing it to us.

"The house is progressing. It gets kind of scary working on the third story which is Duds hideaway. Split palms don't make it rainproof. As soon as a room gets done, we line it with heavy plastic. How long that will last depends on the weather. That's why I want to build a pre-fab house. When, and if we do, we'll all come together. With a pre-fab house we wont' have to rough it as long. This is a lonely place and I really miss all of you. I miss Mark's, "I wanna 'elp you, Daddy." I'd like to give him a hug and rub my nose in his hair like I do."

Daddy's Home At Last

Everybody had their list of things for Harris to do when he got back. Ernie said that he wanted us to go where there aren't other missionaries. He wants us in Miranda for awhile to work with the Terena Indians in that area. One day sitting at the table Melody looked deep in thought and said, "I wish Daddy would come home." Chris took it up right away, "Boy, I do too. Uncle Ernie's coming with the things from Grandma and Grandpa Gregory and we can't open them until he's here." After he'd stopped I turned to Melody and said, "Why do you want Daddy to come home?" just to see what she would answer. She looked at me real disgusted like and said, "You mean you don't know?" Then she said, "Cause I love him – that's why." No thought of material gain: just wants her Daddy home because she loves him. She looked so cute when she said it.

When Harris read that he wrote to his father: "Boy, Dad, you don't know what you missed by not having a daughter. Melody is a little angel who can lift me all the way up. Only a daughter can do that."

On May 14th on our way home from the feira (open air market) we stopped at the post office and there was a telegram. 'Chegarei Quarta—feira as quatro horas. Aviao Missao'. I will arrive Wednesday at 4 P.M. on the mission plane. That was a busy day after three and a half months of planning. You think you've got all your plans made, but when you get right down to it you can think of a lot yet to do.

A little after 3 P.M. we went to the airport with Liz and Ernie. They had just arrived the day before; Liz from the states and Ernie had gone to help her through customs. The Missionary Aviation Fellowship (MAF) plane didn't arrive until after five. The kids entertained themselves well because they had quite a display there; tropical birds in a big screened in place with trees growing in it. There were also tropical animals in a cage and a python snake in another cage. There was a stick by the python cage to rub along the side of the cage. It would start making this horrible sound and then strike at you. It nearly scared you out of your wits the first time. You were really thankful you weren't out in the jungle with it.

Finally the plane came. The kids had been arguing about who was going to kiss Daddy first. When he stepped out of the plane they all ran-away from him. You should have seen him. He had neither shaved nor cut his hair those three and a half months. Quite a change from the crew cut he usually had. It didn't take Mark long to make up his mind. He got the first kiss. Beard or no beard, his Daddy was home!

At the chacara Chuck Harmon had spelled out with white bricks "WELCOME HOME". They saw it from the plane when they flew low to let them know they'd arrived. Also they had killed the 'fatted calf' and so from the airport we went right to the chacara for a churasco. Of course the boys at the Bible Institute had a big time over Harris' beard and hair. He did look awful. It looked as if it harbored a lot of little creatures (bichinhos we called them here). After the churasco they had the chacara prayer meeting. Harris, Liz, Bob Wright (who had come on the MAF plane) and the pilot, Jim Lomheim, all spoke so it was very interesting.

Moving To Miranda

June 7th, 1958. We were all packed up. We had rented a freight car and it had been made up in the freight train. Our car was on top of the freight car packed and sealed and not to be opened until we arrived in Miranda. There are no roads to Miranda.

We had gone there to see the house we had rented and make final arrangements. If the trains are both on time you can take one there, have an hour and a half there, and return the same day. To have more time we decided to take a freight train there early in the morning and then get the passenger train back. I never saw a train go so slow. They said it was over loaded and every few miles it had to stop and work up more pressure. The trip is supposed to take just a little over two hours. We got into Miranda at three-thirty after waiting on a side track to let the passenger train going back to Aquidauana pass us. So we had to stay overnight with Senior Rufo, with whom we will work in the church he holds in his home.

Already we were well known in that area. On the train one man asked Harris if he was going to Taunal. Before he could answer, another man we had never seen said, "No, he's going to Miranda. He's a missionary and he's going to live in the judge's house." Everybody we talked to in town knew more about our business than we did. We must be the current talk of the town.

The house is really nice – only two years old-and being the judge's house carries a lot of prestige with it. He copied it from plans in American magazines. We're paying less rent for it than the one we've been living in. It has 3 large bedrooms, front room, hall, kitchen, dining room, and bath. It has several things most houses don't have here in this part of Brazil: closets in the bedrooms, built in bookcases, built in kitchen cupboards under a sink, and the doors in the bedrooms have a mirror and a drawer that swing out. A big window opens out over the patio. The bathroom has a separate bathtub and shower. The kitchen and bathroom are both tiled halfway up and the floors are all ceramic tile. All the rooms except the kitchen have ceilings.

Also outside there are two nice swings and a see-saw. Chris was overjoyed with the yard. It is full of plants and flowers of every color. The yard is all white sand, but he had put in different planting areas with bricks: different shapes and sizes. There are also little benches and seats all through the yard. It looks like an oriental-garden with all kinds and shapes of pots with flowers in them.

The back part is fenced off and Harris can keep his horse and chickens there. A lot of fruit trees are there: orange, lemon, fig, papaya, and mango. It also has a lot of orchid plants on the trees. He said they bloom in September and October. There's even a place in the back for starting new plants with benches and shelves and a lot of little pots. You can imagine Chris' reaction; he didn't want to leave there to come back and pack. The house is all wired for electricity and for city water but the city doesn't have the electric plant going yet.

There is a well and pump and we can pump water up to a reservoir over the house and have running water inside. There's also a cement patio in back of the house where we can eat outside. It certainly is a long ways from what we thought we'd be going to after language study.

When we got back to Aquidauana we found out the freight car was waiting and we could load it the next morning. The furniture was all crated but there was stuff on top of boxes and last minute things to do. The two girls and Harris and I went top speed all morning and just managed to keep ahead of the movers and by 11:30 the house was empty.

We had left Mark and Melody at the Chacara with the Lubkemans. I guess they thought they'd been deserted. When we didn't come back the same day they decided to take matters into their own hands and started off down the road for home and mommy. Luckily they were missed. Uncle Ernie went and retrieved them.

Before we left our home everybody in the neighborhood came to tell us goodbye when they saw the truck being loaded with our things. Quite a different reaction than when we first moved in and for sometime after. They were really indifferent to us then. One woman even was crying so hard she couldn't talk to us which is really unusual. It made us feel good to know that they had accepted us and were going to miss us.

Miranda and Beyond

The things which you have heard from me among many witnesses, commit these to faithful men who will be able to teach others also. 1 Timothy 2:2

While in the Aquidauana area we never had a vehicle. Just before we went to live in Miranda we were able to buy a Volkswagen Kombi. This means of transportation made it possible to cover the task the Lord had for us. This is a 'bird's eye view' of our ministries in the different areas.

Miranda is a Brazilian town-population 2,000. We concentrated our Sundays in this area with Sunday school and evening services. We had meetings at a nearby farm in the afternoon. On Thursdays we had prayer meetings. There was much Catholic opposition in Miranda. On Monday we had meetings among migrant sugar cane workers (in season), and meetings at a home on the outskirts of town. The owner of the sugar cane farm and sugar factory, who was catholic, asked us one week to go to all of the places where he had workers. He saw that where the gospel was being proclaimed the people worked better, believers were honest with him, and relations among them were better. Semi monthly we had women's meetings. We worked with Senior Rufo, a widower, and his teen-age daughter, Rute, who had a small work in their home. They gave us much assistance. Rute attended the local Catholic high school and received the highest grades in their religion classes. She said she wanted to learn as much as she could about the Catholic religion to be able to answer other kid's questions, and be able to witness to them.

Passarina is a Terena Indian Reservation – population 300. We held Wednesday night evangelistic meetings there with people form Moreira helping us. Some boys from the Bible Institute in Aquidauana were from this village and were a help during school vacations. Liquor had a strong hold on the adults in this area. The Institute boys helped us during DVBS. The chief was not a believer but invited us to hold the meetings in his yard.

Moreira is also a Terena Indian Reservation – population 300. There was an established church there with deacons taking part in the services. Harris had communion there, and oversaw the work. The Christians there helped with DVBS and the children's meetings, along side the Institute students. We did much medical and dental work among these Indians, as well as in the other villages. We helped them through epidemics of gripe and whooping cough. Baptismal services were held here regularly.

Uniao is a private Indian village – population 200. There was a well established church there with a very capable Indian, Sr. Patricio, in charge. Almost everyone here is a believer. The mission owned land there, and they hoped to eventually have a camp there for children and young people of the area. When we were not holding meetings, doing medical work or visitation, Harris was building, digging a well, or planting in Uniao.

Cachoeirina is also a Terena Indian reservation. With the Volksy, we were able to have meetings there Friday nights with the members of the church in Uniao in charge. We helped with music, lights, and transportation. Very few there understood Portuguese. We were so thankful that the Indians there could hear the Word of God in their own language through Sr. Patricio and others. The Carregados (heads of the Indian Protection Service) were very encouraging of our work in Cachoeirina. There were no professing Christians at first, but we always had very good attendance at our meetings, usually about 100. Boys from the Bible Institute held DVBS there also, and helped in the work.

Learning from the Nhambiquaras

Missionaries had worked with the Terena Indians for many years. They had established schools and a Bible Institute. Its graduates were going into their various villages to do the work that we had been doing. Some of them even had hygienic and medical knowledge. The Lord had been showing us what was to be our work in the future among tribes who hadn't heard about Jesus and His love for them.

The Nhambiquaras were a nomadic Indian. They would visit the Funai Indian Protection stations on a temporary basis and did the same when the missionaries, who couldn't live on the Indian Reservations, settled nearby. Guapore wasn't on a reservation and didn't have a Funai station in their area. It was hoped that all the tribes in the area would come to the new station. They could work with them while they were there. This did create different problems. You had complete responsibility for them while they were with you: You had to feed them, treat them, give them work to do. They weren't above stealing from you. When groups of twenty or thirty of them were with you they could eat a lot. When they had been wandering through jungles for days or months they could have a lot of medical needs. They also wanted to earn things while they were with you so you have to provide work for them.

One day when Dotty Kinsman and I were alone at the station, we went to check on the ones who were working in the roca (gardens). We found everybody eating and nobody working. Some were eating our yucca we needed for their meals. They had roasted it over a fire. Others were

roasting rats that they had captured. Some were eating caterpillars they had found on tree webs. They were all enjoying honey they had dug six feet down to find. Dotty said in exasperation, "We're paying you for working and nobody's working. Everybody's eating!" One old woman looked at us and said, "You eat when the sun's here and here and here and all day long you do dishes. We eat all day long and we don't have any dishes." We had to laugh and I turned to Dotty and said, "Who is the smart one here. I don't think it's us." That old Indian woman was so funny with her motions getting her point across.

Our children and I had flown from Cuiaba to this new station where Harris had built the Kinsmans house. Dud Kinsman had gone to Cuiaba to meet Harris and they had gone down with Dud's truck to Aquidauana to get our possessions. It was five weeks before they arrived back at the station. Our baggage and Volkswagen had been shipped by train, with us on it too, from Miranda to Aquidauana. We had spent that night shuffling from station to station dropping off other train cars. Then we had traveled rough roads in the Volkswagen the long road to Cuiaba. It was very interesting, but also very tiring. The road had ruts for trucks but the wheel base of the Kombi didn't fit and we had to make our own path through muddy roads and mountains. We almost lost the cages of the pets that were on top of the Kombi at one time. Our children got a science lesson from a large boa constrictor that had been ripped open by a passing truck.

When the first group of Indians arrived at Guapore, the children and I had come a couple of week before. The women all had a dress on. The oldest one, Alice, just had on a dirty t-shirt. The men were naked except Padre. It was our first encounter with wild Indians. There is something about their dark skin that almost makes it seem as if they are clothed. They were all healthy looking; it really surprised me how well formed their bodies are. Their hair is the most repulsive part of them. They hardly ever attempt to comb it. I wonder if you could get a comb through it. They're always wiping their greasy, dirty fingers in it and of course it is full of lice and their nits that serve as another form of food for them.

The men wore a reed through a hole in the center part of their lower nose. They also had a coarse straw in a hole in their lip. Most of them

had large ear rings. They also had tight arm and leg bands woven from grasses. They usually wore some kind of necklace made from seeds, feathers of pretty birds, parts of insects and who knows what else. We would trade for these and pet animals with tiny glass beads. The women loved to make necklaces of those for themselves and their children. If the necklace broke or they spilled them they would want to find every lost bead. They painted their skin red at times with urucum (a red berry) which served as a kind of bug repellant. The borrachudas were very tiny blood sucking insects. During the day we tried to keep covered with heavy cotton stockings and pantaloons, long sleeves and pants, as much as possible, in spite of the heat.

As soon as they arrived, Coracena took them to a place where there were a lot of grubs (large worms) with big black bugs mixed in. They would turn over a log and, presto, dinner. They came back with a bucket full. They tussled with each other over them and ate them raw, dirt and all. Coracena is a Nhambiquara who had been with Dotty for several years. She knew what they liked. She had also cooked them hard field corn. They took off the outside part of each kernel before they ate it.

Bernice had a baby about six months old and she fed it by chewing the food herself first. Then she put the baby's mouth to hers and spit it in.

Padre was crippled and his legs bothered him a lot. He and Vincente, the oldest Indian in the group, appeared to have had polio we suspected. They were both lame and their legs were deformed. Padre asked Dotty for medicine and when she gave it to him he pulled down his pants and rubbed it on the sore spot. Melody was quite shocked that he didn't have underpants on. The naked ones didn't seem to bother her. But since he had pants on when he came, it just didn't seem right for him to pull them down without undershorts. Some of them were very adept at stealing, so bore watching.

Their houses were just crude triangular huts open at each end. They sat and slept right on the ground so they were often very dirty. But they were a very good natured Indian and you learned to love them in spite of the dirt.

The front of the Kinsman's house had been built as a hanger for the MAF plane when it was there. It was also a storage place and provided shade for the Indians to eat and to hold meetings. At noon we gave them one plate of food. Then we would have a meeting with them during the hottest part of the day. After the meeting they could have a second plate of food. On Sundays we did the same with breakfast and supper. They usually went hunting after the meeting on Sunday morning. On Thursday nights we had a culto (meeting) before we gave them their food. That way we had good attendance at our meetings. No one got food unless they had worked, except at breakfast. They were surprisingly respectful in meetings. We knew they were not understanding everything and tried to make it as interesting and simple as we could. They loved to sing and were usually smiling and laughing.

On cold nights I felt for them sleeping on the ground in their birthday suits. They did keep fires going around them most of the night. That helped not only to keep them warmer but keep them safer from wild animals, bugs, insects and vipers.

When the men finally arrived they brought news that the heads of stations were to come to Cuiaba right away as the director of our mission was to arrive for special meetings with them. We had also received word that a sick Indian wanted us to come to his village and get him and his group. So Harris put our Volkswagen on top of Dud's truck as the cut off to the village was quite a ways down the road. So Harris and Chris left with the Kinsmans and I was left with Mark and Melody in charge of the station. I counted on Corecena helping me, but she had a miscarriage soon after they left. The Indians were still with us. It was only for a few days until Harris came back with 21 Indians, the barrel of gas, 4 dogs, numerous parrots, and lots of their snacks – those worms and bugs all over. They had hit a stump in the road going in to find the Indians. He cut down a tree and fixed it good enough with that to get home. It was two months until the Kinsmans returned. Dottie had phlebitis and they went to Annapolis to a hospital and the doctor they trusted. Harris was able to get our house built enough to live in before they came back. This was in spite of Sue having an attack of appendicitis, settling Indian fights, giving medicines to Sue and the Indians, directing food preparation for everyone and keeping the Indian's working.

When Dotty and Dud came back they brought Joao and Jose with them. They had studied at the Bible School in Aquidauana for a couple of years. Jose was young, probably ten or eleven, but smart as a whip. Joao had been a real help in the work. Ruth Harmon taught him to play the organ and harmonica. He had a good singing voice and could serve as interpreter for the other Nhambiquara. He was a nice clean looking boy and a real contrast to the other Indians. Joao and Corecena were married. He had gone with Dud on the truck when they went to get our mudança.

Usually Saturday nights we had a playtime with them. They loved to run races, sack races, wheel barrow races, bow and arrow contests, musical chairs, dodge ball etc. They don't understand all the rules usually and they got into some funny circumstances. I think we had as much fun and laughed more than they did.

This is what they taught me:

1. Nhambiquaras were just like us – people who God loves and died for.

2. They have the same basic needs as anyone.

3. They knew if you really liked them and were concerned about their welfare.

4. They'd test you to see if you meant what you said.

5. Not knowing their language was a real barrier. You couldn't expect them to learn your language. You had to learn theirs to understand them. Their language was a tonal language and one of the most difficult of the Indian languages in Brazil.

6. You needed interpreters to help you in the beginning and even later.

7. You're more easily accepted when you go in as a family. Children can be a great help in the ministry.

8. You had to learn to laugh and live together.

9. Those who have never heard of Christ won't live up to Christian standards.

10. We learned new ways of doing things to be more effective.

11. Missionary life is also transient. You go where you think is the greatest need and where you can be the most effective.

12. It's being what God wants you to be, and letting Him do His work through you to bring them to a saving knowledge of Jesus Christ.

SECOND TERM
1961 -1966

Parecis Indians

Life with the Parecis Indians was very different than with the Nhambiquara. We were living at their village and many of the things that distracted us among the wild Indians were taken care of by the Parecis. We could spend more time studying the language, having school for them, teaching them sanitary measures and the value of money. Of course, our spiritual ministry was always our top priority even though it was at the bottom of the list Funai wanted us to do.

The Parecis were semi-civilized but that didn't mean they were easier to work among. They had accepted many of the vices of civilization. Missionaries who had traveled through their territory to reach the uncivilized thought they would be very hard and hard-hearted to work among. When they traveled through their villages they said they were liars and tried to steal everything they had. The missionaries would go off into the wilderness to get away from them to camp for the night.

These Indians live on the Serra dos Parcis which is a plateau approximately 2000 feet altitude. There were at least 15 villages along the 100 mile stretch of a branch of the Pan American Highway. Their villages were scattered over an area the size of the state of New Jersey. The road followed the continental divide of Brazil. The headwaters and rivers on one side flowed north to the Amazon River. Those rivers where we settled were crystal clear. On the other side they flowed south to the Paraguay River. While we were camped out in the tent, Harris had surveyed the area and picked a location in the middle of this territory on the Sacre River for us to locate.

Most of their homes were large communal houses with several related families living together. They first made a framework and then tied palm branches to the poles with vines. There were no windows except where people had wanted to see out and had pulled aside a palm branch. There was a low door at either end. Inside it is just one big room. They all sleep in hammocks the women have made from strings of small palm-like plants. The hammocks are hung every which way. It is like a maze to get through. The women are very adept at making the hammocks. It 's an interesting process to watch. Clothes are thrown over ropes or vines which add to the maze.

High tables are here and there with small fires burning underneath. On top of the tables are large pieces of meat being cooked and smoked and balls of massa. The massa is made form the roots of the manoic (cassava) plant which the women pull from their fields. The roots are from 12 to 24 inches long. After washing them in the river they peel and grate it on a grater made from kerosene tins.

There are two kinds of manoic: One type they bake in a fire, boil it in a pot, or make a stew out of it with bits of meat. The other type has a poisonous liquid, prussic acid, that can kill or make animals or people very sick if they prepare it like the tame type. It's not easy to tell the two types apart. They prefer the poisonous one to make the massa for their bread. They wash the grated root of the manioc bravo and then squeeze out as much of the liquid as they can with a cloth or woven mat. Then they form it into balls and put it over the fire to dry out. It has a slightly sour taste. I grated the tame manioc and made it like a pizza. It was very good. To make their bread they crumbled some of their massa into a big frying pan to brown and cook. Sometimes they would make it thicker and cook it right on the coals of the fire.

Their fields are usually a ways from their houses. They cut down the larger trees and then set fire to the whole area. I have never seen a fire burn out of control. There are marshy areas around the higher ground that control the fire. That also gives them the advantage of not having to water it.

As the fire burned, the Indians, Harris, and Mark would have target practice with bows and arrows and guns shooting snakes, rats, poisonous centipedes etc. running ahead of the fire. The fire burned for days and also did away with ant's nests and other insect pests. When the fire burned out they would plant the manioc stalks and corn among what was left. The logs they would later cut up for firewood.

Mark was the hunter of our family. At an early age he was very adept at swimming and handling arms. The Indians would often come running for him when they saw an animal or bird they wanted him to kill. Sometimes his curiosity would get him in trouble when he would bring home little ocelots or jaguars for pets. He soon learned that the mothers would hunt them down.

There were lots of deer and emu (ostrich) in this area. We never lacked for meat. When we eventually brought children from other villages to study in our school we always had meat and fish for them to eat with the manoic we bought from the Indians.

When we came, none of the ones in our village knew how to count, read, or the value of money. They got victimized when they went to buy anything because they would hand over all of their money and let the person take what he wanted. They also used the bills to wrap around tobacco they grew on a small scale. It didn't matter if it was a 100 or 500 cruzeiro note they wrapped the tobacco in to smoke.

They had feasts to honor their gods. A great deal of preparation would go into the feast. They would hollow out a long log and then they would chew the grated manoic and spit it into the log. It would be left to ferment for several days. They also sent out hunters to gather in a lot of meat. Parecis would come from many of the villages. They all brought their guns and there was much gunfire during the celebration. They had a small tree planted in the house. They split the ends of the branches and had home grown tobacco rolled in cornhusks in between the split ends. They bring out their flute gods from the flute house and the men lock arms and do a little jig back and forth. Some of them sing in a three tone monologue while the flutes play. The women never take part in this. They all hide in one of the houses. Their tradition says that if they see the flutes and the dance that they will die within the next year. Sexual orgies do go on during the night we've been told.

The indigenous Indians were considered half citizens. It was against the law for anyone to sell or give them liquor. When they would come back with a bottle of liquor Harris would pour it out on the ground. They didn't like it but they knew it was illegal for them to have it. They probably continued to bring it back but we never saw it. We could tell it by their actions. It did help to curb drinking in our village and usually their drink was enough for them.

As Harris visited these villages among them for the last time before furlough, there was a note of sadness as they questioned, 'When are you coming back? When will you start school for the children? Won't you build your home in our village?"

Harris was on his way into Cuiaba for the birth of our fourth child. I had gone into the city by plane before he had left the station among the Nhambiquaras. Rebecca Ruth, Becky, arrived before Harris and Chris did! Two months after her birth she was on her way to the states in an Indian basket with a lid on it. That basket served her very well for traveling.

"Camping Out"

Arriving back in Brazil after our first furlough, we found out that our Volkswagen, house and belongings were at an abandoned station. The Kinsmans had moved from there to a more advantageous location among the Nhambiquaras.

Before leaving Brazil, Harris and the Field Committee had decided when we returned, we should move among the Parecis Indians and open a new work among them. They were 250+ miles from Cuiaba on the Serra Dos Parecis. This is a Mesa the size of the state of New Jersey. The Parecis are a semi-civilized Indian and no missionary had had a concentrated ministry among them.

Harris and Chris flew up to the Guapore to get the "Volksy" and survey the situation. Flying over the roads they could see that they were badly deteriorated. Previously we had planned that the children and I would stay at the old station while Harris surveyed the area of the Parecis. Due to the condition of the road and the abandoned station we realized we had better stick together.

In the end we were invited to live in our tent, temporarily, at a new station where Wycliff Translators, Orland and Phyllis Rowan, had recently gone in to begin translating the Parecis Language. When we were in language study in Aquidauana, Geddy Strickland had just moved out of the small house on our property. Orland was surveying another tribe near Miranda. Phyllis had a new baby so she lived in the small house while Orland surveyed that tribe. Later they had a house in Miranda and they lived near us there. We were surprised, but very pleased to hear they would be working among the Parecis too.

The tent was hurriedly set up. The children were left in the care of the Rowans. Harris and I went on the MAF plane to retrieve what we could at our old station. We had previously arranged for a truck to pick us up later.

The house had been put together with screws so we were able to bring back pretty much everything except the adobe. Harris had contracted with the Parecis men to build us a Pau-pique house (their kind of house) for our storage.

They put a large tarp over the tent which made it much cooler. The Indians wove panels to protect the sides. The tarp and panels extended out front. This made a protected area for cooking, eating, studying, teaching, visiting, worshipping and just living. The tent had two zippered compartments for sleeping and a storage area for supplies. It was up off the ground on a wooden platform. We usually had an audience. When we laughed, they did too. They tried to figure out why we did what we did. We sometimes felt like animals in a zoo with crowds watching us. Our school sessions could get quite interesting.

But what better way to get acquainted then being right there with them. So this was 'home sweet home' for awhile. We actually lived like this for almost a year before we moved to our permanent location. That was true camping out.

Psalm 32:8 "I will instruct you and teach you in the way you should go; I will guide you with my eye."

Organization 1961

Living in a tent for over a year had its ups and down, especially for Chris. He was twelve and needed to be kept busy when he wasn't studying. He had gotten several model kits when we were in the states and often asked, "Where can I make models?" The answer was always, "Chris we're not organized." After that his favorite quotation was, "When are ever going to get organized?"

Harris decided to help Chris out and organize at least one part of our lives. He got busy and took one of our packing crates and put hinges on the bottom of one side. Inside he put all kinds and sizes of cubby holes. A large clasp and padlock protected Chris' treasures and models from curious fingers. When the lid was down it was a combination worktable and storage place. When he was working with his models he had plenty of observers. But at the end of the session the side went up and everything was safe.

It's just like life. We often can't get organized completely, but we can often organize one part and make life smoother. I was thankful I was married to an organizer who was always looking for better ways of doing things.

When we moved to the new station Chris met another problem when he started planting a garden. He had gotten the Gregory Florist blood in him following his Grandfather around the greenhouses and fields while we were still living in the states. Behind our house, fields of flowers stretched over to the greenhouses and his grandparent's house. We encouraged this interest as fresh fruits and vegetables would be a welcome addition to our diet at our new station.

Harris got fruit trees and seed for him. He worked with him in laying out a garden. As soon as the tender leaves appeared so did the carregador {leaf cutting} ants. In one night they would strip the leaves off a tree or do away with every evidence of a garden. They used sprays and fogging poisons but it seemed the ants came from miles around to feast. Chris replanted time after time.

Harris got a novel idea of using a blow torch. He would go along the path of the ants like a fire-eating dragon. Sometimes they would go a mile or more to find their nests deep in the ground. Then they would use the foggers and poisons until all of the entrances were found. It was hard to believe how big one nest could be. This was virgin territory and those ants had gone unopposed for centuries. But gradually there were fewer and the plants and trees began to grow. They still had to make nightly excursions to check on ants for some time. Until Chris left for school in the states he kept us supplied with fruits and vegetables.

We moved our chicken yard deeper into the woods as our flock grew. The fenced in one near our house was turned into a garden and produced many vegetables. It had the advantage of being near our water tanks that were filled nightly when the generator was running. They were high up in the air and we could water with a hose. Chris' efforts did much in keeping us healthy.

Sometimes our experiments back fired. When DDT was first packaged in little cans that you could squeeze, we used it to kill lice in the hair. We didn't realize the dangers of it until we used it in buggy corn we were feeding to our chickens and baby turkeys. All our little chickens and turkeys began shaking and dying. We even had a couple of our little emus die.

One of our blue and yellow macaws took one of the sick chickens under his wing – literally. He would caw and it would come to him and he cuddled it under his wing. It would stay there shaking from the effects of the poison all night. At first toward evening, we would let the chickens out of the pen for a while to eat the bugs around our house. As darkness approached the macaw would take the chicken to the fence, climb it, and call for the chicken to follow. Finally he would climb down, put it under his wing and take it into the pen. How often we thought of the hymn 'Under His wing I am safely abiding'. It was amazing to see the concern of one type of bird for another. When the chick finally died the macaw would try to get others to come to the shelter of his wing, but in vain. How we wanted the Indians to learn about our loving heavenly Father, who wanted to shelter them from their fears and vices.

Waya-Aka Beginning

Soon after we moved to Waya Aka, in my Sunday School class among the mothers and their little ones, we had a lesson on heaven. Later Becky asked me if her house in heaven would be made of adobe. She was helping Jose mix the adobe mixture, as only a two year old could. After living in a tent for over a year she thought our new house was wonderful. For days afterwards we would chuckle when we thought about Becky's adobe mansion in heaven.

Harris finally decided on the location where we would locate our new station. It was in the central location among the Parecis villages on the Sacre River. As the Indians visited us they would say in their language,

"Waya Aka". ("This is a good or beautiful place.") So we named it that.

We had enough cement to do a cement floor for the kitchen. The rest of the floors downstairs would be made of adobe.

To our surprise, we received word that our home church in New Jersey had sent us a gift from a legacy of $1500. It came just at this time when we were trying to cut costs to fit our budget. Instead of boards for windows we could plan on metal frames and glass jalousie windows. We went ahead with adobe walls as they were partly up. Harris had constructed the house so that in the future we could replace the adobe with bricks. He knew the adobe was inferior {not the right type of mud in this area}. It was already washing away with the tropical storms and wearing away where the Indians leaned in to look through the dining room slide window.

The second floor had boards cut from the trees in the forests nearby. We got fine sand from the river and gravel from a gravel pit found near the house site. The rains were making the boards curl in places so they cut thicker ones which solved that problem. We had aluminum roofing we'd brought down from our house in the Guapore. It had nail holes in it but he hammered the holes shut as much as possible and used washers where they were needed. The pressed board did for the inside partitions that had been the outside walls at Guapore. The frames and the glass for the windows each cost $100. That we could afford now. We also could cement all the first floor as well as make porches for the front and back doors. Eventually we hoped to cover all those floors with tile. How we did rejoice at the Lord's provisions right at this time of construction.

In the midst of this, a large group of Indians arrived from another village. They wanted to stay and earn supplies. They were needed help at just the right time.

A short time later the plane arrived with the field director and his wife, Tom and Betty Young, and a young student Gracinha from Jacutinga, a Brazilian Bible Institute. We hadn't expected her to come so soon. She had asked us if she could come and help us with a Daily Vacation Bible School. We weren't at all prepared. But on the same plane we received supplies for a DVBS that had been mailed from a church in Manasquan, NJ over a year before. All the things that we would need: construction paper, stories with figures, crayons, papers with pictures to color and things to make and do.

The Youngs wanted to see some of the other villages. While Harris took them Gracinha and I planned the DVBS. At each village he picked up children so they could be at the DVBS. "All things work together for good." Harris also brought Benjamin – the most progressive man among the Parecis. He had Bible studies with Benjamin and Jose, our most faithful worker. Both of them accepted Christ as their Savior during the week.

So our DVBS far exceeded our expectations with children from our three villages, those who had come with the workers from the other village, and those picked up on the Young's trip. Without communication you have to be prepared for anything.

A lot of mouths to feed and a lot of work keeping the construction going, DVBS, Bible studies, and struggling with the language. Our first attempt at a DVBS among the Pareces Indians, totally unprepared for, but the Lord had it all planned. We wondered if the food we had on hand would stretch, but deer meat was plentiful and the Indians kept us well supplied with manioc from their fields. It was more of the Lord's provisions. It was wonderful in our eyes from beginning to end; especially as we saw the first fruits of the Lord's work among the Parecis. Always before when groups from other villages came there were rumors and accusations, fighting and distrust. We saw the Lord working in hearts and there was co-operation and harmony.

Exploration near the Galera River

By G. Harris Gregory

Pushing forward into new areas in order to reach the unreached for Christ was ever the object in mind as we tried to search out the different Indian tribes. Thus Robert Wright, a fellow missionary, five Parecis Indians, and myself left by truck from Waye-Aka for the headwaters of the Galera River. Later that day we arrived at a supply camp of those who hunt ipecac in the region. Here I left the truck in the care of two Parecis. After talking that night with men who were acquainted with the area and approximate location of some of the Indian villages, we decided to go in a northwesterly direction to contact a group closest to the Pan-American Highway. Our purpose was to find a group with a good location for starting a work in this area.

The next morning five of us started out on foot. We followed the ipecac hunter's trail at first and then an Indian trail. The first day we passed our last source of water at noon and did not reach the next river until the following morning. The first night was really dry. The rest of the trip we had water, but always drank sparingly because of the uncertainty of the distance to the next river.

Late in the afternoon of the third day of walking we came upon Indian gardens, old and grown over. We were all anxious to reach water that evening so we continued farther until suddenly we came out onto one of their present gardens. As it was just getting dark it was too late to attempt to enter the village. We camped in the woods nearby and found water flowing through the middle of the garden. We reckoned that we were about 700 meters from the village, with woods and a valley between us. This was too close for comfort, so we decided not to make noise or build a fire that would reveal our presence. Once in a while we could hear them yell, a dog bark, a child cry, or wood being chopped.

Just as I was climbing into my hammock at about 7p.m. one of the Parecis men heard bird and insect calls in the jungle and said that a hunter returning late must have seen our tracks and cut off the path to signal others. He was certain these calls were man-made. He wanted to run back over the trail, but I made him realize that he had heard the calls in that direction also and that we could be ambushed at night very easily. Also if we did retreat we would be afraid to come in the next day for fear they might be waiting in ambush.

I decided that we should stay right where we had camped and show them we were friendly. We built a fire, big enough for any close Indians to see; we also hung up hoes, bush axes, and knives on a line near the fire to display them. I played my harmonica softly and we did not talk too quietly. We called out Parecis words such as 'friends', 'presents,' etc. when we heard a close sound. I wanted them to know that we were not trying to sneak up on them, but at the same time did not want to alarm the village nearby.

Needless to say, we did not sleep much that night. We had prayer with our Indians but still two of them went a short distance back in the woods and hid. Bob, Jose, the third Indian who was a believer, and I took turns attending the fire all night. As the night wore on and I paid close attention to the calls and noises, I was convinced they were not made by Indians. As it turned out they were not.

It started to get light at 4:30a.m. and we broke camp at 5. Cautiously we followed the path through the garden without event. Not a sound had we heard and I was thinking that possibly the villagers had fled during the night. We then sighted their houses and a dog at the edge of the clearing. We passed the dog without it making a sound, which was very unusual. We could not see or hear anyone from the two big houses. I went forward alone and when I reached the center of the clearing between the houses I shouted, "Anybody home?" in English. A man stuck his head out of the small low door. He came out bow first, followed by other men with their bows and arrows. I laid down my gun to show them this was a friendly contact. I offered them a small bag of sugar. Right away they brought manioc root to us. The captain, one of two with some clothing, indicated that he had a sore throat and I gave an aspirin to him and one of his two wives. I offered them water but they just chewed the medicine down.

The other Indians did not speak one word of Portuguese or wear any clothes, not even a string or a decoration. A woman came out so I opened my can of glass-seed beads to show them. Then the Indians really came alive. I told them the beads were for the women. The men called the rest of the women and they came out with gourd containers for the beads. The others in my party joined me without incident.

The Indians were very friendly and hospitable. Joe took scissors and cut the other Parecis' hair. They were very interested in the scissors and wanted their hair cut too. They all had short hair and they showed us how they cut it with clam shells.

They took us into their houses and offered more food which we accepted and ate. The houses were very dark inside and I used my flashlight to see. They were very interested in that too. In one house we could not stand upright as there was a second floor that was packed full of corn. Their gardens were huge. They looked healthy and strong, some my height and shorter. The women have good teeth, but the men do not. I believe that was due to their constant smoking of green tobacco.

That same day one of them led us to another village 25 minutes away. Only three couples were in that village at the time, as the others were away hunting. There were thirty people in the first village. Two of those were from another village farther away. We also learned of two other villages in another direction.

There was not an elderly Indian among them. They all were under 30 years of age. They resembled somewhat the Nhambiquaras, but we later learned the two tribes are afraid of each other. They do sleep on the ground and puncture the center of their nose and upper lip and rub charcoal on their faces. They worship the bamboo flute and have a flute house. They do not seem to be nomadic.

They were the most primitive Indians I had ever seen. One of them we called the caveman. The trees in an old garden were cut down with fire. They planted with a stick that looked like a canoe paddle. In the village there was just one broken knife and one axe. They liked sugar but not salt. When I took out a sack with salt written on it to salt the meat they had given me, I knew they thought it was more sugar. When he insisted, I finally gave it to him and tried to explain how to use it on the meat; to just sprinkle a little bit on it, not to put handfuls in their mouth like they did with the sugar. When he stuck a handful of the salt into his mouth he began sputtering and spitting. I got tickled and laughed, which was the wrong thing to do. He grabbed one of his arrows (fortunately not a poisonous one) and lunged at me with it. I jumped back but he did make a scratch on my stomach. I shook my head and indicated no in sign language. I took a fistful of salt in my mouth and spit it out like he did. He laughed at me and I demonstrated again how to use sugar and salt. They never did ask for salt. It was unknown to them.

They were interested in looking at our 22 rifles, but didn't have any idea how to make them go off. Of course, we did have the safety on them so there was no danger of harm to them or us. Most wild Indians know only the shotgun. They just shook them and pointed them in different directions and soon lost interest in them. I had pictures of my family and tried to explain the camera to them but they were never really interested in that.

As I sat in the captain's house I began to play my harmonica. After just one song he wanted to try it. He blew a bit and then made a sign that he wanted it and offered me his bow and arrows. We also traded 2 axes, 2 hoes, 2 bush-axes, and 2 knives. They seemed to know what to do with those tools as they had looked all through our sacks without stealing anything and asked for just those. We received from them 5 bows, about 25 arrows, 2 sacks of manioc stalks, and a half bushel of soft corn for planting.

There was a very good spot at this village for an airstrip so I marked one out and they started to clear it. After three days we were quite good in their sign language. They did not catch on to giving us the nane of things. They just repeated everything we said. Even when we repeated their language incorrectly they did too. The third day at the village the Indians led us to the highway. It was about a five hour walk through scrub woods and fields. I considered the trip very successful. Truly the Lord blessed and prepared the way.

Measles and Whooping Cough Strike

Missionary life can go along pretty much the same, day after day, in a calm routine. Then all of a sudden everything seems to happen at once.

Harris had just returned from a successful search in the jungle for unreached Indians of the Galeira River area. There he located two groups of very primitive Indians. The Lord had prepared their hearts as their past reputation was not too good. They received them well and were very friendly.

Now it was time for our Daily Vacation Bible School. Gracinha, the same girl who taught last year, came here again this year on her Christmas vacation from Bible School. School started off fine and Harris went to other villages to bring more children. In two villages he found sick children. One baby had already died. Some had whooping cough and others had measles. Mixed in were some who had TB. In the past, measles had meant only death to the Indians. They have no resistance to it and get pneumonia because of the way they treat the sick. He could not leave them to die so brought them back with him, families and all.

We kept the sick visitors isolated on our side of the river. Our plans changed from one to two Bible Schools, one for each side of the river. When he mentioned this to the people across the river and that the sick ones were at our house, panic struck. Consequently, they all moved down river until the disease passed. We still had two Bible schools; one for the well children and one for the well but contaminated ones.

We treated with injections, cough medicine and vitamins. Praise the Lord that no one died here. The first group recovered but when he took them back to their villages, as well as the children he'd collected for Bible School, he'd find more sick and bring them back. Some families had lost three or four of their children. They arrived by foot, too, carrying one child in their arms and another sick one on their back. Some came before their children were sick saying that it was easier to bring them while they still could walk. We had groups of twenty-five from one village and thirty from another. Some with just measles, others with measles and whooping cough and we tried to keep them separated from each other. We had them in the garage, in the school house, and under tarpaulins. Not only did we have to tend to their medicines and shots but also feed all of them. Harris kept after the men to go hunting and they kept us supplied with meat. We used three sixty pound sacks of farinha (manioc grated and dried) and several sacks of rice and beans. We had a lot of squash from Chris' garden which was a help. So gradually they would get better and group by group they left – and others arrived.

We praised the Lord for His provision of miracle drugs that really did perform miracles on the sick ones. Some of those who died in the villages we had seen recently. You could hardly believe they could die so quickly. I really believe that if it weren't for us being here most of them would have died. I'm not saying this to be bragging because nobody knows better than Harris and I how little we could have done without the Lord's help. We believed that the Lord was using this sickness to make the Indians more conscious of death and its consequences and also to build up their trust in us. We told them they didn't have to die from measles and we've proved they don't. Now when we tell them you have to believe in Christ or you're eternally lost they can't help but remember that we don't lie to them and we care about them. That's the purpose of all this medical work right now.

Nobody from our village here got sick. They did bring all of their children back for the immunization shots Harris brought back from the city for whooping cough, tetanus, and diphtheria. They had a diphtheria epidemic in the city and they said that it would also help those who got whooping cough to have a lighter case. They all looked so healthy and well, but their attitude was bad. The captain, Urivado, sent word to Harris that he was to send all these sick ones away or they were going to leave this village. So Harris sent his regards and told him goodbye. He said if it was their village that needed treating he'd do the same thing for them. If they needed help they would get it. The rest from this village assured us they would come back as soon as the sick ones left.

So our plans for a Daily Vacation Bible School ended very differently than we had planned. We knew we would be busy with the children but we didn't realize what else would be involved. Gracinha was planning to go into Indian work after her graduation and had certainly had a taste of missionary life with its heartaches and victories.

Victory Through Tragedy

Brazil, G. Harris Gregory

On a Sunday afternoon in the middle of our two weeks of Daily Vacation Bible School came the news: Benjamin is dead! It came to us as a great shock.

My thoughts immediately went back to a year ago at this time during DVBS. Benjamin, our first convert, had accepted Christ just a short time before, and was here for the study of the Word. I had special classes during that time for him and Jose, also a new Christian. Benjamin was known and respected by all in this area. He was the captain of the most advanced village and looked up to by all the other Parecis. He treated everyone fairly and conscientiously, and I never heard one word spoken against him. He lived his Christian life in the same manner.

Upon receiving the news of his death, Sue and I went the next day to his village to comfort his wife. How we praise the Lord for her testimony. She had accepted Christ just 4 weeks before, one week before Benjamin went on his trip. Just before he left, she said, he had told her if he should die before she did, to notify me and to do as I said. He also said not to destroy anything of his except his clothes, and to turn everything over to me to handle for her. It is the custom of the Parecis to dispose of all the possessions of the deceased. They do not want remembrances of the dead to be around. Also from past experiences with death, I have seen the relatives of the deceased carry on insanely for weeks, stricken with grief.

Dona Juvantina, his widow, was sad and broken up over his unexpected death. When we entered the house, she flung herself in Sue's arms and cried. She was understandably heartbroken, and we felt helpless and sad ourselves. I had prayer and Bible study with her and the others there, and explained to her the truth we have in Philippians 1:21; how that Benjamin was happy and rejoicing right then with the One who died for him. How wonderful it is to see these primitive people, without an education, leave their heathen ways and accept God's Word. She calmed and collected herself marvelously after this, and explained all that Benjamin had told her before the trip.

She asked to see the grave and I took her there. Benjamin died while returning from the woods, still two days by foot from his village. A trucker took the body to the nearest settlement where he was buried. Benjamin and three others from his village, together with a civilized Indian from another tribe were returning from an unsuccessful hunt for ipecac in the deep jungles. Their Indian companion seemed happy and harmless, but unknown to them he was a wanted killer. He kept asking for bullets, and finally Benjamin gave him two. Then one night, stealing a pistol, he fired a shot at Tenorio, another of the Parecis Indians. The bullet missed Tenorio, but hit Benjamin in the heart as he approached the campfire. Tenorio, after carrying the news to Benjamin's wife of his death, had come directly to our house to inform us of the tragedy.

We are all sad because of his sudden death, but the Lord knows why, and we know that it was not in vain. Benjamin's adopted sixteen year old daughter, Youvonne, accepted Christ that Sunday evening in our meeting. Tenorio also accepted Christ at the same time, as did his wife the next day.

We do pray that the experience will be a means to make the Parecis think seriously, and that these new believers will continue to grow in God's grace. Dona Juventina, being a new Christian, asked with some doubt about burning candles. She is seeking to do what is right in the sight of God. I showed her in the Bible that Jesus Christ is the light of the world and He is our light. I told her that nowhere in God's Word are we instructed to burn candles for the dead.

Benjamin was captain of only a small tribe of Indians, the Parecis, poor and uneducated, but he had obeyed God's commandment that we should believe on the name of His Son, Jesus Christ. Because of this belief, the Bible teaches we can be sure that this day he is enjoying the beauty of Heaven and fellowship with His Lord and Savior Jesus Christ. Pray that other Parecis Indians will remember the challenge of his life and testimony, understand the salvation that is in Christ, and their responsibility to make a decision for Him.

Reinforcements

On one of his trips into the city for supplies, Harris met a German fellow, Sr. Edmundo Zonar. He and his wife, who was Czechoslovakian, and their seven children had had an unfortunate experience. A man who wanted to start a settlement of immigrants hired them to clear land and start preparing the area. It was in a very isolated part of Brazil and the man left and never returned. They had no money and little food and almost starved to death. Both Sr. Edmundo and Dona Ida were Christians and Harris hired them to come up and help with the building up of our station. Sr. Edmundo was a very talented and dependable person and his three older sons worked well with him. Harris could give him instructions and go on about his own work. They were a wonderful help in the construction of different buildings we needed; a church, dormitory/school, garage/workshop, storehouse, a house for their family, and three small houses for visitors.

Harris had bought a form in the city for making cement blocks. The first thing in the morning he would make 50 blocks out of a sack of cement, sand from the river and gravel from a gravel pit near our house. The Indians and even Sr. Edmundo couldn't seem to learn the knack of getting the blocks out of the form without breaking them. Tito, his Indian helper, would have it all mixed for Harris, which was a big help.

Edmundo was very good at sawing boards from the trees that had already been cut down. The sons would take turns at one end of the saw with Edmundo at the other end. So the building up of the station went much faster with the family and the Indians working.

Dona Ida was also a big help in the house for Sue. She helped with cleaning, meal preparation, sewing etc. When school finally started, the younger children of the Zonar family attended the school we had for the Indian children. We were glad we could meet that need for them.

One day Melody and the oldest Zonar girl, Lori, had put a board over a wooden fence and were see-sawing. Melody was heavier than Lori and she came down hard and Lori fell off. She landed on her arm and it was broken. It looked like an S instead of straight. I told one of the brothers to go get their father. I needed help. Sr. Edmundo was digging a latrine at the time for the dormitory. He wasn't sure how he got out of that deep hole, but he came running. I was just ready to tell him the story when he took her arm and gave one jerk and it went back straight perfectly. We couldn't believe it. We took apart a crate and used the boards for a splint and wrapped it tight. We all knew that the Lord had performed a miracle for us. As far as I know she never had anymore trouble with it.

Christmas came shortly after they came to live at Waya Aka. The Zonar family had few possessions. They only had one fork which they passed around while eating. We went through our barrels and supplies and found clothes, household goods, toys and food for them and wrapped them all in Christmas paper. When we carried the packages over to them on Christmas morning they were overwhelmed. It was a wonderful time for our family too as we experienced the Biblical principle that it is better to give than to receive.

They participated in our church services. We praised the Lord for their time with us. Again we saw the Lord providing for our needs abundantly above what we could ask or think.

In Brazil if you have someone working for you over a year you have to give them health insurance and also retirement benefits which we couldn't afford. So before the year was up we took them back into Cuiaba. With the money they had been able to save while working for us, they got a lumberyard and sawed trees into boards and sold them.

School for the Parecis

School! This word was unknown to Parecis children and many of their parents. They have never had the opportunity to go to school. The Padres had a school at Utietiti for Indian children of various tribes. But they said they have given up on the Parecis Indians. The few that they had taken from their villages had either run away or proved impossible to teach. To us the reason for this is that no Parecis group can get along with those in any other of their villages. They seem to be constantly spreading lies and stories and everyone is ready to believe anything. They blame sickness or death on witchcraft of someone in another village and relatives seek revenge. Their life is constantly one of fear and hate. For this reason opening a school for all Parecis was not an easy undertaking.

The Lord wonderfully provided a teacher for us, Gracinha. For the past two years she had taught in our DVBS. The Lord definitely answered another request for a dormitory supervisor and cook. Dona Felicidade, a widow in the SAM Cuiaba Port church and a dedicated Christian, had been praying for an opportunity to move and enter into fuller service for the Lord. When I presented the need to her she gladly accepted without hesitation.

Sr. Edmundo completed the dormitory, school and church building in April and we started school for the children in May. One side of the dormitory was the kitchen and apartments for Dona Felicidade and Gracinha. The middle part for dining was open on the two outside parts. The other side was divided into dormitories for the boys and girls.

The children received a Bible lesson every day at school and another every open evening for devotions. Susan also directed a sing time. Wednesday was a Bible Study and prayer meeting for all. Friday night was game time. Twenty-three children enrolled with fifteen of these living in the dormitory.

Many came from other villages and stayed several days working or visiting their children. Some of those in the "uttermost parts" were hearing and believing on our Lord Jesus Christ.

We believe that the school was the most effective and lasting way to reach and hold the Parecis for Christ.

Becky's Desire to Serve the Lord

When we visited my sister, Janet, in Bolivia, it turned out to be a very profitable time in Becky's life. The week after we got back to Waye Aka, Becky said to me, "If Vilma can teach a Sunday school class, why can't I?" Vilma was the little Bolivian girl there at Zapaco that taught their Sunday school class. Vilma was just a little older than Melody, and Becky was quite struck at having their playmate teach their class. It took me quite by surprise, as she was under five, so I said to her, "Would you like to teach a Sunday school class?" It was the first time that any of my children had expressed a desire like that. Melody and Mark had just recently started to pray in prayer meetings. I didn't want to squelch a desire like this.

At the time, I was teaching the women in the dining part of the dorm. They all had little ones that were under school age. At times it was quite frustrating, as the little ones would lose interest when I talked to the mothers, and would be very distracting. I told Becky that she could take the children in my class and teach them in the girl's dorm, which was right off the dining area. During the week I would teach her the story she was to teach, and ways to apply it. On Sunday, I gave her the papers we had prepared on the story and crayons or scissors. I also gave her a bag of cookies, candies, or popcorn to give them if they were good. Positive reinforcement! We also took a low bench in for the children to sit on. It really made a difference in my class, and I could concentrate on my Parecis and teaching just the women. Of course, the kids loved having their own class in their own language. It is amazing how children pick up languages.

Several Sundays later, Harris had a bad cold, and most of the men had gone on a fishing trip. Harris eavesdropped to see how Becky did. He said she did well. She ordered the kids around like a general – "You sit there. You be quiet" – as only another child could do. She did the class in Parecis, and the kids were understanding it, answering questions, and paying attention. The only criticism he had was that she taught sitting in the hammock, so at times the children were straining to see the flash cards. We had to work on that.

She continued to teach for a couple of months. All of a sudden one Sunday, Becky decided that she wanted to hear Mommy give the lesson, so we joined classes again. I continued to teach and prepare her, though, and by popular demand of the little ones, she continued with her class.

Not long after that in prayer meeting, all of the school kids were praying, and she whispered to me, "Is it all right if I pray?" Of course I told her to go ahead and pray, and she did.

That was the beginning. Until she was seventeen and went back to the States, she always had her classes. Not just on Sunday, but whenever we visited any of the villages and even in our own village. She would ask for story material, take the children off under a tree, and tell them stories and teach them songs. Later on, Melody began making up songs in their language. Each of my children were so different. Becky's teaching had a real influence on the Indians growing up. Soon some of them would tell us after school vacations, "I taught the kids in my village just like Becky did," and we began making materials for them to use.

Alinor

No one could have foreseen what God would do with a single life spared from the ravages of a deadly disease. He had work for the Lord to do.

After the completion of the dormitory/school Gracinha returned to teach in the school for the Parecis children. Also a deaconess, Dona

Felicidade, from the church in Cuiaba, came with her little adopted son to supervise the children in the dormitory and prepare their meals.

One of the older boys among the first students was a boy called Alinor. Alinor proved to be one of the brightest of the group and would quickly finish his lessons the teacher gave him. Then he helped the younger children in their own language to understand the Portuguese. He had a very good disposition and was willing to help others. He was one of the first to accept Christ as his Savior.

We would just hold school for two or three months and then have a month off so those from other villages could go back to be with their families. During that time Harris would make exploratory trips to find or visit other tribes to open up work for other missionaries. We would also go and spend time in the different villages of the Parecis. We would put up the tent there and live with them awhile. While there we would hold services, teach the children that were too young to come to our school, hold children's meetings, do medical work, pull teeth, etc. We also took things from our store to sell. Sometimes Harris would take his chain saw along to improve the roads, cut down trees for firewood or to make their gardens.

The Parecis men and older boys would go off into the deep woods along the river between Bolivia and Brazil to gather a plant called poalha (ipecac in English) during some school vacations. Poalha is a plant that is used in making medicines against vomiting. Harris would take the plants into the city and sell them for the Indians. The poalha grew in marshy areas. There were many dangers and unhealthy living conditions and it wasn't unusual for some of them to come back ill.

One year they had been gone for some time when one of the boys came to our place. He was panting and very tired. We could see that he had been running for a long time. "Come quickly, Senior Jorge. Three of the boys are very sick. The men are carrying them out to the road. They want you to come with the truck so that you can treat them here."

When they got back it was obvious that they were very sick. They seemed to have exploded inside and had high fevers. They carried them to the village, put them in hammocks and put cans under them to catch the blood. Within half an hour one of them had already died. We knew they all would die unless we got them into the city right away. Before my husband could get everything ready and the truck gassed up to go the long way into the city, the second one was almost dead. They wouldn't let him go into the city.

Just Alinor was left to go. His father, Sabastiao, hung a hammock in the back of the truck and laid Alinor in it. He went with Harris to tend to his son along the way.

After the truck left they came to tell me they were taking the other boy down river to die and be buried. I went with them to the place where they had laid him down on the path. It was dark and with my flashlight we could see that he was covered with ants. They had placed him in the carregador ant's path. We did our best to get them off of him and they continued down river.

The Indians didn't want to hear the names of those boys. They loved to see photos that we had taken of them, but they said, "Don't show us any photos. We might see those three boys who died and it would make us cry and be sad." We told them to pray for Alinor so that he wouldn't die. But they said, "No, he's already dead."

When Harris got to Cuiaba with Alinor and Sabastiao he went around to all the hospitals trying to find someone who could treat a very sick Indian boy. This happened when the Indian Protection Service was changing to Funai (Fundacao dos Indios) so it wasn't operational yet. Finally a doctor at the cancer hospital agreed to try and save his life. He admitted him to the hospital. He said he had no idea what it was after he heard the history of the three boys. But praise the Lord, Alinor lived and apparently had no ill affects from it after he got his strength back.

When we wrote to the states about it, Harris' folks happened to see an article in the New Jersey newspaper on Bolivian Hemorrhegic Fever that people were dying from on the Bolivian/Brazilian border. Several doctors from the United States went to investigate it and one of them had died. It said that it was related to Lassa Fever in Africa with many of the same symptoms. They thought it was probably spread by rats.

That would explain why none of us or the other Indians got it We tried to take every precaution but we did wonder if others would get it.

We had no way of communicating with the city. Three weeks later, when we heard the truck's horn far away, everybody came running over the bridge from the village. When Alinor jumped off the truck there wasn't a dry eye. "We thought you were dead" everybody said to Alinor. "No, God saved my life for a purpose. He has things for me to do."

God did have things for Alinor to do. After he finished our school he went into the city to help Orland and Phyllis Rowan in the Bible translation work. He graduated from the public school there and also from a Brazilian Bible School. He continued with the translation work. Later a Brazilian church supported him and also gave him a truck.

He served his people and won some of them to the Lord.

In other villages our students are also teaching and holding meetings to tell their people how much Jesus loves them. Thanks to the Rowans they now have the New Testament in their own language. Orland went to be with the Lord but Phyllis continued to work on the translation of the Old Testament here in the states with occasional trips to Brazil.

THIRD TERM
1967 - 1972

Life is not Simple

All was ready. We had just shipped our International truck with a camper on top and personal belongs to Brazil. We thought we had all the proper import papers and there would be no problems. How wrong we were.

We flew into Campeinas airport. We had been invited by Milly and Harry Bollback to stay with them while Harris got our things out of customs. Susan was over six months pregnant. We had left Chris and Melody at Ben Lippen High School in Asheville, North Carolina. Just Mark and Becky had returned to Brazil with us.

When Harris presented the papers at the Alfondega (customs) in Santos they told him it would take a week to ten days. He did need the Bill of Lading, which unfortunately was back at SAM headquarters in Lake Worth, Florida. This was the first delay.

While Harris waited, he stayed with and helped in the ministry of Pocket Testament League in Santos. They had a sound truck and showed movies and preached in the different bairros of the area almost every night and handed out New Testaments and other literature.

They finally told him he could not import the vehicle under the law we were using. The mission did not fit the requirements. This required a trip to Rio to see what the problem was. They suggested another law to use to bring it in. Under that law the charge would be at least a million cruzeiros. In addition every day you leave it in customs you're charged a fine for not claiming the vehicle. We didn't have that kind of money, even though the price would be less than buying a similar vehicle in Brazil. Even so, he returned to Santos with every cent we had.

He subsequently made several trips to Rio besides continuing to work on it in Santos. Our prayer warriors and we were praying. Harris had also been trying to contact a friend from Cuiaba, Sr. Rondon. He had been the head of Customs in the area at one time and had helped others with their problems. Rondon's wife had informed Harris that her husband was in the area. The Lord performed a miracle and Harris was able to contact him, finally. With a phone call, Rondon was able to open doors and accomplish what we couldn't. He even went down to Santos to be sure that his orders were carried out.

We only had to pay for the paper work and the "despachantes" fee (the man who Harris hired to help with the process). All this occurred over a period of two months. I had told Harris he had better read up on delivering a baby as the time was drawing near.

The day after they got the truck out of customs was Sunday. All of us, the Bollbacks and others, piled in the camper and crew cab to go to church. As we pulled up to the church one of the PTL fellows came running with a fire extinguisher in his hands. Dark smoke was billowing out from under the truck. They yelled for everyone to get out and they streamed out of the camper and cab.

We sat there dumbfounded. Harris was exhausted from the whole process and now it was going up in smoke. Finally they got the fire out. A chain they had used to lift the truck into the hold of the boat had dented one fender and must have damaged one wire going to the camper for the fan over the stove and to the water pump. Maybe the weight of all the people had made the difference. Harris had just driven the day before up the mountain to Sao Paulo without incidence. But it couldn't have happened in a better place, where it was detected even before we noticed it. Shortly after that we were traveling on a rugged lonely road into the interior.

We had less than two or three weeks before we had to go back into Cuiaba for Lance's birth. I know the Bollbacks must have been thankful to see us go after two months. They had been wonderful though and I tried to help them in various ways while I was with them.

Lance – God's Gift To Us

You formed my inward parts. You covered me in my mother's womb.
I am fearfully and wonderfully made. My frame was not hidden from you.
When I was made in secret your eyes saw my substance, being yet unformed;
And in your book they all were written. The days fashioned for me, when
as yet there were none of them. ~ Psalm 139:13-16

On January 11, 1968, the Lord gave us one of the biggest blessings of our lives. He gave us Lance Victor Gregory. He was born in Cuiaba, Mato Grosso, Brazil, in a new maternity hospital still under construction. It wasn't long before we realized he was a hemophiliac. Since it had been in my mother's family and is inherited through the female we knew there was a possibility of me being a carrier of the gene. Since we already had four children with excellent health we even had remarked that the Lord knew we couldn't continue as missionaries with a hemophiliac. The Lord was going to show us that with Him "nothing is impossible."

As he grew there were bumps, bruises, swollen arms and legs. We'd try to figure out what happened and not let it happen again. When he began to crawl and walk he started biting his tongue or injuring other places in his mouth.

After he'd bled for a week at our yearly Brazil Missionary Conference we decided he should go to the states to see what could be done for him. Since Susan was behind in home schooling the other children, we decided it would be best for Harris to take him. Our parents were all in Florida and they were a big help to him.

Sue's parents were members of the Hemophilia Society in St. Petersburg and the Society helped in making arrangements with the Crippled Children's Society to help with expenses. He was admitted to All Children's Hospital for testing. While there he developed his first joint bleed in his knee. They diagnosed him as missing factor 9 or Christmas Disease. We didn't realize it was a misdiagnosis until 12 years later.

The factor 9 concentrate had just come on the market. It had to be kept frozen and kept on dry ice and hand carried. As we used it we realized cold compresses or keeping the bleeding place in ice water worked better than the concentrate. Also, there weren't that many missionaries coming to keep us supplied.

The Sacre River that flowed past our house was 67 degrees year round and he loved sitting and playing in the water. Our children and the Indians would entertain him there. The women washing our clothes in the river would watch him with their own children. The Parecis were very good with him. They knew he bled freely and took every precaution with him to avoid it. He grew up with our family and the whole tribe of Indians protecting him.

At first we made emergency trips into the hospital in Cuiaba to administer the injections into the vein. His blood vessels were extremely tiny and even the Nuns, who were very experienced, would often have to try several places. But soon Harris learned how to do it and took over giving him the injections. But Lance had a real love and affection for those Nuns who in his own words said, "they are the nice ladies who gave me my injections," when ever he saw them.

One missionary conference we went to Bolivia to join with the Bolivian missionaries of SAM for conference. On our return we had bought a small fan to install in the cab of our truck. It was Easter weekend and the custom man told us we would have to wait until Monday to go through customs with that fan. I think he kind of liked that fan and was hoping we'd say, "Keep it". But we'd already reserved our flight for all of us on the plane the next morning. I tried to explain to him that our son was a bleeder and he needed blood and it had to be kept cold with dry ice. I mentioned it was in the styrofoam container. He went to examine it. When he stuck his hand in it he quickly drew it out because of the cold. He again asked, "What's in there?" I said, "blood concentrate". I went on to explain his condition and why he needed blood. And it had to be kept on dry ice, etc.

It was late at night and Harris was holding Lance. We thought he was just tired and he really looked like he was ill. We found out later in the hotel he really was ill when he "up-chucked". The customs man looked back and forth from Lance to the container. Finally he pushed everything over including the fan and said, "You can go." When he went to get the papers I said to Harris, "Saved by the blood. Thank you Lord."

Missionary Kids

I've heard it said that missionaries are called but their children are drafted. God's word tells us God's opinion of all children. In Psalm 127:3-5a, "Behold, children are a gift of the Lord; the spirit of the womb is a reward. Like arrows in the hand of a warrior, so are the children of one's youth. How blessed is the man whose quiver is full of them."

Every child is different. To a missionary family their children are very important to them. Decisions about housing, schooling, all phases of rearing a child have to be carefully considered. Along with being responsible to God for the ministry He's given to them, they are responsible for their family and the many decisions that have to be made to coincide with their work. There is a special connection among missionary families and in Brazil the missionaries were all called aunts and uncles by the children. Some single missionaries were very close to the children and were really appreciated in the input and influence they had with them. When the Lord entrusts you with a special needs child you can either look on it as a blessing or a hindrance.

Lance was a definite blessing to us. The extra attention he required made you so thankful for the good health of your other children. It also made a special bond between Harris and I with him as you were constantly aware of how dependent you were on the Lord for his care and healing. We learned to take him as our 'pillar of fire by night and our cloud by day.' As the Lord led the Israelites he led us to special ministries when Lance had good days and I, Sue, had to be ready to limit my activities when he had needs.

But we found our children a wonderful contact with those we were ministering among. A lot of our work was with children and children are always watching families and their interaction. Becky's starting to teach a Sunday school class at an early age was a wonderful example and the school children doing it in their own villages showed them they could do it too. When there was work to be done our children would mobilize their friends to join in. I once remarked they're either going to be generals or chiefs. At missionary conferences we sometimes had to intervene as there were all chiefs and no Indians.

Melody was a favorite of the Parceis girls. They would get their heads together and compose songs and choruses in their language. The older girls would play with a younger sister on their hip. No one was left out. Even Waxidya, whose name in Parecis means garbage, who had a hare lip and cleft palate, would take her hand off her mouth and play happily, except if strangers were around who wouldn't understand she was just one of the group. When we'd go on a walk down the road or through the scrubland or jungle with Lance someone was always willing to carry him.

Mark had special abilities in the water and with a gun. From an early age he was like a fish in the water. For awhile he would rescue me from going down river by grabbing my hair and pulled me to land. His father had warned him not to let me get near him or we'd both drown. Often the Indians would call him to shoot a bird for their supper or spear a fish for them that they'd seen in the clear water. He was the hunter and fisherman of our family.

All of us used snorkels and flippers and the Indian children lost their fear of going into deeper water when they could see clearly what was around them in the river. A lot of the activities of the school children centered near the Sacre River with its diving board, ropes from trees, tower and castle Harris had made from leftover cement blocks from the construction of our station.

Our location was also an attractive place for retreats. Young people came from Cuiaba during Carnival to have an alternative from ungodly activities in the city.

Near our house along the river was a slope with large boulders for sitting. Groups would hold meetings there. It was especially effective at night when they would build a bonfire on a level place right near the river. They often would have a testimony time there after the meetings.

We also had three groups from Sao Paulo come and camp between our house and the river. Missionaries and business men came as chaperones with teenage boys. One time they came in a PTL (Pocket Testament League) truck and showed movies for all of us. They enjoyed seeing Indian life at our village and the primitive Galera Indians that Harris had contacted. They also showed the films at other Parecis villages as well as for a road crew that was working on the branch of the Pan American Highway near Rio Verde.

When they returned to Sao Paulo and showed the movies and slides from our area, one of the mothers and the wife of the head of the American Embassy in Sal Paulo came for a visit. We were amazed sometimes at who appeared at our door or on the road as we traveled. We thought we lived in an isolated place but our area attracted many types of people. We were also a popular stop for other missionary families going in to Cuiaba or returning from there. Our children looked forward to these visitors and joined in their activities.

School Improvement

The oldest daughter, Leozinha, of the people who had the pensao at Rio Verde lived with us and helped in the school while the other teacher was in the city. Her two little sisters, six and nine, came with her to go to school. Harris did most of the teaching to show her how to do it. He discovered that the other teacher was letting the kids do what they wanted when they wanted. He gradually turned more and more of it over to Leozinha but rigidly oversaw it. You might call it Gregory's Military School. Harris was a great disciplinarian. But the children seemed to be taking it well.

When we came back from the conference most of the Indians were off at a big fiesta at Benedito's village. Evidently even the men who profess to be Christians took part and danced. When Harris corrected them and told them that a Christian shouldn't take part in anything dealing with other gods, which they already knew, they got angry and said they wouldn't let the children come to school anymore; but the next day here were all the kids for school. Parecis spoiling their kids worked to our advantage that time. The captain told them not to come but the kids insisted they wanted to come. So the school went on as usual. The children are really the hope of the tribe.

I could see a real change for the better just since Harris took over the school. They could read phonetically before but didn't understand what they were reading. So he took them way back and explained practically every word they use. Also in the Bible class he repeats, repeats, and repeats until they can answer questions. This hadn't been done before. Often when they prayed you couldn't exactly understand what they wanted to say – much of it was parroted phrases. But now their prayers are showing they're really thinking what they're saying and they make sense. I can't say Harris was crazy about teaching Indian kids – after telling them 15 times the same thing he's sometimes ready to pull out his hair. Well, maybe that's what he needs too: self-control and patience. We need the Lord's help to see the needs of the people around us and then how to care for those needs.

Blessed are the eyes which see the things that you see,
for I say unto you that many prophets and kings wished to see the things
that you see, and did not see them, and to hear the things that you hear,
and did not hear them. ! Luke 10:23-24

Village Life

During school vacations we visited different Indian villages. The camper was a terrific help with this. Harris spent most of the day with the Indians in their houses; hearing their language and learning more of their beliefs and ways of thinking. He found that talking with individuals and small groups accomplishes much more than holding meetings for all. We did have an evening meeting but there always seemed to be so many distractions and you wondered how much was being taken personally. When you are talking to one individual they know you mean them.

Becky enjoyed singing and telling stories with flashcards to the children. We marveled at her eagerness and that she received so much enjoyment out of doing this. She did everything in the Parecis language and had a real concern for the Parecis children. One night I went into her bedroom and she was laying there crying. When I asked her what the matter was she said, "I was just thinking about the Parecis and how they will go to hell if they don't learn about Jesus. They just don't seem to understand." We're so thankful for her concern.

School went on as usual for Becky no matter where we were. Being shut up in the camper with Lance gave added distractions. His favorite pasttime was winding my clothes line around posts and handles on the floor of the camper. We felt like spiders waking on his web. There's also the excitement of trucks whizzing by on the highway. Lance took watching at Indian villages. They are notorious for their broken glass and rusty tin cans, broken bones, and mean dogs. Lance has the normal interests of a two year old and kept me hopping behind him. Lately he had had a bad knee – bruised due to his hemophilia. It seems to be always getting re-hurt in spite of an elastic bandage, sponge-filled leather kneepads that Harris made, and long pants. Even that doesn't slow him down. He's a constant source of entertainment for the Indians—and us—and their way of life is a source of entertainment for him.

Like Becky we sometimes felt frustrated. Just how could we reach the Parecis with the gospel? Just how can you get people interested in eternal values when they aren't even interested in bettering themselves? Civilization was reaching them but the only parts of it they were interested in is what comes easily. Very seldom does a truck get by without several of them racing out to sell their artifacts. Those living along the road were not poor: they have more money than most Indians. The only part of education that interests the adults are prices and how to count your money. We needed wisdom day by day that our time among them was not wasted. They are souls for whom Christ died and He has commanded, "Go ye into all the world and preach the gospel to every creature." Mark 16:15

Visitors

While living in a very isolated part of Brazil, the Lord gave us many opportunities to witness to others besides the Indians.

Among the missionaries who traveled on this branch of the Pan American Highway we were the closest to the mission home in Cuiaba. We brought barrels of gas up on our truck for the MAF plane to refuel. Due to the fact there was no radio contact we never knew when that would happen. But we did enjoy the mail and fresh fruits and vegetables that came up on it.

Also, the other missionaries that lived further on down the road would often stop in and sometimes stay overnight. AS the Indian work progressed among other locations, the wives and children would stay at our station during the exploratory contacts.

Amazingly, people on foot appeared on our doorstep: some strange, others barefoot, a teen age girl. The chief of police came investigating mistreatment of Indians by the ranchers. Peace Core workers and Funai (the Indian Protection Service) came with medical teams to test the Indians. People came to test the soil. A group of bridge builders came and built a bridge downriver from us. Harris helped with the underwater construction.

These groups often came ill-prepared to live in the wilderness. We helped them with supplies and fed them when we could. Groups came who were exploring Brazil or traveling around the world. Most of them would stay and work on their cars or trucks, using Harris' pit and tools. One group of just girls' had overturned on the road above us. Harris worked on the car enough to get them into the city.

Another group came looking for a fellow who had been at our place a month before taking the census. They couldn't find him, but they had found out that he missed a lot of places. That young fellow had been sent up in our vast area on foot to accomplish his job. The priest brought him into our place, but he was just hitching rides – no wonder he disappeared. The new group retook the census. They didn't have any food with them so we fed them and kept them overnight.

Each one that came was an opportunity to show Christian love, concern, and witness to.

Fourth Term

1973 - 1978

Fourth Term in Brazil

City living in Cuiaba, Mato Grosso, was very different from life in the tribe among the Parecis. Our first problem was finding a suitable house at a price we could pay.

Gracinha, who had helped us in the work among the Parecis, and her family had two large rooms on the front of her families home with 20 foot ceilings. There was no place to go but up. Using his ingenuity, Harris put the girls' bed up on poles, with a ladder, in the dining room. Underneath the bed were a desk, dresser and closet. Across from their bed was a buffet and on top of it at bed level was a lazy-Susan with bananas on it with a rat trap beside it. When the girls heard the lazy-Susan start to spin they would cover their heads with the sheet until they heard the trap shut. Sometimes they'd forget, and the rats would get mixed up with the barrels of supplies behind the buffet until we smelled them.

You see the house was made of thick adobe and it was a row house with common walls and roof. The rats played tag on the rafters from one house to another, and oh, how they loved bananas. We could watch them from our bed and hear them in the night. So our bed and Lance's had a canopy over it just in case the rats should tumble.

Lance's car-bed, Harris had made for him, had an engine compartment filled with pajamas, elastic bandages, syringes and concentrate as needed. Along with our bed his was up on a platform with stairs leading to it.

Beneath it was our dresser along with tables and supplies for the classes we had with women, children, and students who showed an interest in what we were teaching them in English and Bible.

Mornings, Harris taught math in the Wycliff/SAM co-operative school for MK's, including Becky. Lance continued studying with me at home, as he would have been the only one in his class in the Wycliff school. Afternoons and nights Harris taught English and Bible in the Brazilian High School to all ages of students.

You can take a person out of the jungle but you can't get the jungle out of them. Especially when God has given them a story to tell of how he has worked in their lives. This book is the story of God's plan for our lives. You can imagine how people were curious about these Americans with two blonde girls and a little boy who always wore knee pads living in this strange home. They'd never seen anything like this. They watched us like the Indians had. Our only window was right on a narrow sidewalk on a busy cobblestone main street. We couldn't live with the window closed. So our lives were open to the public – but what better way to get acquainted with passer-bys. The only entrance to our home was down a long hallway leading to the family's patio and living quarters. Oh how we got mixed up in their lives while living with them in the same house. That is another story of God's Plan and how He worked in our lives to reach other people.

God works in mysterious ways his wonders to perform. Again we had to admit it wasn't our will to live in such a place but His will was best for reaching the people he had for only us to reach. Harris was also in charge of the Port Church, SAM's missionaries had established.

As I said before, these row houses had a common thick adobe wall between them. One morning, after several days of heavy rain, we heard a terrible noise. When we went to our one window and looked out the air was full of dust and rubble. After awhile the atmosphere cleared. When we went outside to see what had happened we could see that our common wall with the house next door was still standing. But the walls of the next two houses had completely collapsed and the houses were just a pile of adobe, roofing and household goods. How thankful we were that our wall had held.

Not long after that the mission asked us to move to the dormitory for the children of missionaries living in the tribes. It was just partly constructed and they wanted Harris to continue with the construction. The couples with children to live there were all on furlough, so our living quarters changed again. It was closer to the school for missionary children. Also two newer SAM couples lived across the street from the dorm – one on either side. Harris helped Jim and Gloria Young build a mobile book store in their van to reach out in other areas with Christian Literature. We were also very close to a new University and we had a Bible Study in the dorm for interested students. We found that a very fruitful ministry.

Calamity by Fire

The day started in the water and ended in the fire. At Waye Aka the safest place for Lance had been in the Rio Sacre. Lance really missed the river when we moved to Cuiaba. The Cuiaba River is s silt-filled dirty river and you can't see anything in the water. In contrast, the Sacre was crystal clear and although there were caimen and boa constrictors you could see them in the water and keep track of them This river was not one to swim in or get in your mouth. But he did enjoy playing along the edge and imagining what dangers might be there.

When we got home, Sharon Stillman, a single missionary we called our "Thursday family" because she usually came on Thursday for supper, was there waiting for us. She had come early to visit with me and had been waiting for an hour. While I was talking to her and starting to get supper ready, Lance ran out back to see what the neighbors were doing and to tell them about his adventure in the Cuiaba River.

Dona Maria had been cleaning up her yard and was burning palm and banana leaves. Lance climbed up on a mound of dirt to watch it burn. As he was coming down he slipped and his left hand went right into the fire and also the side of his left leg. A repeat performance of what Mark had done a few years before. Imagine how we felt when we saw him. He was really in pain and kept saying, "Everybody, all of you, do everything for me you can. Will you? Help me!" His fingers looked like balloons.

Harris had just gotten in from teaching his afternoon class in the public school and, of course, we did do everything possible. We mainly just kept the burnt parts in ice water. Harris had to go back to the Brazilian school again to teach Bible at seven and I still had Lance's hand in the ice water when he came back at eleven.

The poor kid really did suffer, but we were so thankful that we just had burns to treat and no trouble with bleeding. With him, of course, that was a big concern. I guess the fire had sealed off everything. We kept it all covered with carbolated petroleum jelly and antibiotic salve and gave him antibiotics internally.

Needless to say a good part of my time for the next week was pretty much taken up with him. I read more to him, spent more time playing with him and treating the wounds. Fortunately it was his left hand so we could go on with school and he could do drawing that took his mind off of his pain. So that crisis passed. We had a lot to praise the Lord for. It could have been much worse.

One of Becky and Lance's Summers in Brazil

What do MK's do when they are on vacation during the summer? It varies for all of them as there are many opportunities to travel and see interesting parts of their chosen country. This is an account of one of Becky and Lance's summers.

One year at the cooperative school in Cuiaba they gave the teenagers a chance to earn extra scholastic points. They got one hour of credit for each one hundred hours of service helping others. They didn't get paid for it. The parents helped with transportation if necessary.

Some weeks Becky worked twenty hours helping Jim and Gloria Young in the Christian Bookstore in downtown Cuiaba. She enjoyed helping them so they could do other things She liked meeting people and having the responsibility of helping them. It taught her a lot about dealing with a business and answering questions.

She also planned our meals and did the preparation and clean-up. This included everything connected with it; like going to the open air market and stores to purchase what she needed. She sewed school clothes for herself. In our home she helped me clean, wash clothes and iron them.

It also included Becky spending time with Lance and Trina Young, while her parents were at the bookstore. When she did that she had to plan activities with them and tell how they behaved, if she had any problems, and how she was able to solve them.

Lest you think we took advantage of her, she learned a lot. She had fun and felt good about herself. Since we had moved to the dormitory for SAM's MK's, we were close to the Wycliffe Chacara. She went out there on her bicycle and they would reciprocate and come to our house. On Saturdays they usually had some activity planned with one of the teachers or parents. Sometimes it was an overnight camping trip or a nature walk. The Gladfelters were teachers at the school and the kids loved him teaching them about the flora and fauna. There were various mountain streams in the area around Cuiaba and swimming was a favorite sport on those trips. They also continued to form musical groups and perform in churches and homes.

Lance was also busy but he did have problems at times. One time he was recovering from a bleed in his upper right thigh when he hurt his left ankle. The first time the Irma (Nun at the hospital) went into the vein the butterfly needle clogged so she went in again on the same hand. The first hole must have seeped for awhile as that hand really swelled up. He still wasn't walking because of the ankle, but some how he hurt the big toe on his good foot so that was bothering him. Harris would sit up with him and tell him stories until he got sleepy. As long as his mind was busy he was fine, but when he lay down to sleep it throbbed and needed Tylenol or something stronger to make him relax. He did a lot of teeth gritting at night.

In spite of it all he did keep himself busy and us too. The radio set that Harris had brought down years ago was a big help. Harris put it up for him to play with – complete with portable aerial, headphones, and microphone. He imagined all kinds of things. He also got absorbed with encyclopedias. He had a good selection with all of ours and also the dorms collection plus all kinds of used school books.

He also had friends come in and play. He loved having the Snyder boys come – usually one at a time. He called them "Dave's boys". He made comic books about the "Hair Force" to entertain them. It was like the air force with little hairy men and their adventures. Another friend was Leissa Rowe who was a little older than he was. The Rowes came for supper and their younger daughter and Lance had a good time together. Leissa was born with a club foot and had had several operations so probably understood some of Lance's problems better than others. She loved to "imaginar" and she and Lance hit it off.

One day in school as Sue was attempting to define "handicap" for Lance she mentioned that perhaps you could call hemophilia a handicap. His reaction was, "Well, I don't think it's so bad. There may be some things you can't do, but there sure is a lot you can."

As we looked around us and to the ministry the Lord had given us we too realized that we are sometimes handicapped. There were some needs we couldn't meet and some jobs that we wondered how we could ever accomplish. We realized that in our own strength it was impossible. We had to leave them and the results with the Lord to accomplish in His own way. His Word has promised that, "I can do all things through Christ who strengthened me." Phil 4:13

MOVING ON

Eleuthera

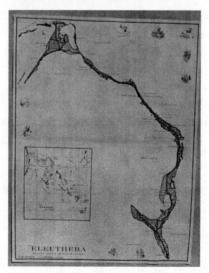

Not far off of Florida's coast lie the Bahamas Banks. Out of them rise more than 700 islands and islets with inviting beaches of pure white and pink sands. From the air as you fly over the shallows it is breathtakingly beautiful. Miles of sweeping swirling sands are punctuated by green slashes where deeper waters have cut a pathway.

This was an entirely different path than we had expected. Out of the jungles of the Indian work and heavy schedule of city life in Cuiaba, we moved to a beautiful tropical island. While on home ministry as we studied God's word, prayed and considered our family's circumstances, God led us to one of the westernmost out islands, Eleuthera. Since SAM only has work in South America we changed missions to Gospel Missionary Union.

Windermere High School was the focus of GMU personnel on Eleuthera. Our responsibility was mainly in the outreach on the southern part of the island. Its modern history began with the settlement of the 110 mile long island by a group of English adventurers seeking religious freedom. Freedom is the meaning of Eleuthera. Most of the island is one to two miles wide and five miles at its widest point. The language is English with some quaint changes so no language study was necessary.

The waters of the Atlantic Ocean and the Caribbean Sea almost come together at the Glass Window, a natural wonder on Eleuthera's northern tip. On one side of the Glass Window are the crashing waves of the dark blue Atlantic. On the other side is the calm turquoise water of the Sea.

Our home was high on a cliff overlooking Tarpum Bay, a typical Bahamian settlement, and the scenic Bay. Harris built Lance a two story tree house with a 'look-out' where he could see both sides of the island. It was made with relics found on the beaches: planks of a certain wood found only in Brazil, nets, ropes and other things.

Our work was mainly in the settlements of Green Castle, Wemyss Bight, Deep Creek and Bannerman Town with another missionary, Annetta Loeppky, helping us. It included visitation, Bible Clubs in the schools, youth meetings in churches, Bible Studies, and checking correspondence courses. Becky came during her school vacations from Miami Christian

College and nurses training at Dade Community College to help us in the ministry. Harris' part grew to include Theological Education by Extension with leaders in the churches, and classes at Windermere High School to train the students to help us in the out reach.

There was a great need for Christian literature on this island. We had started this by having a book rack in the super market at Rock Sound. Harris made a model of a mobile trailer we could pull behind our car and take literature to all the settlements on the island. We submitted it to the Mission Committee at Miami Christian College. Praise the Lord that it was chosen as their project during their missionary conference. We brought a utility trailer with us when we came and they paid for Harris converting it into a Book Mobile. They also furnished some books and teaching materials to equip it.

In a survey we made we found a church in Green Castle that was all but closed. Harris was working with the leader in the TEE program to build up the church. We had a Sunday School there as well as youth groups.

After ministering in Brazil for twenty-one years, it was good to have visitors from the states to help us in the outreach ministry here. Harris' mother was able to spend part of the year with us after the death of his father. His brother, Eugene, and his wife, Betty, also came. He was a pastor and chalk artist. He presented chalk drawing programs with musical tapes and preaching in six different groups, drawing 2 or 3 pictures and presenting them to the churches. The students at Windermere School also enjoyed his presentations.

Becky and a singing group called "Serenity" came from Miami Christian College. The chaperons for the group were the head of the Missions Department, Rev. David Aszbach, and his wife. He spoke in the ten different meetings we had on the island and also had a class on missions during Windermere's Spiritual Emphasis meetings. The speaker for the meetings was Dr. R. Melick, also from MCC. We were thankful for the impact their dedicated lives had on the people.

One of the outstanding youth groups that came to help us with DVBS was a youth group of forty from St. Simons Island, Georgia, led by Bill and Ida Walker. They brought a large yacht with all the materials for teaching and crafts as well as all the food for their group and us. The boys stayed on the yacht at Davis Harbour and the girls stayed with us and in the Goddard's house here in Tarpum Bay. During their time here we held VBS in three settlements: 165 attended in Greencastle; 75 in Deep Creek and 90 in Wemyss Bight. Becky was here on vacation and also participated. Part of each day in addition to their preparation sessions, they enjoyed swimming and spear fishing and exploring the waters in boats. Each evening they conducted their own spiritual growth sessions. Some of the group were relatively new Christians. We rejoiced to see their growth in just one week; many of them realizing new talents and experiencing a new love for others very different from themselves.

Then a week of preparation for more Vacation Bible Schools: This included training sessions too. This time students from our own GMU High School volunteered to help. While some GMU staff held them in settlements to the north, we were assigned Bannerman Town in the very south and Tarpum Bay where we lived. The total attendance for these two was 167. Again, many came to a saving knowledge of Jesus Christ.

You never knew when you would have an exciting adventure here. When Mark and his family came to visit, it seemed as if the water was full of sharks. Everywhere they would go they saw them. Many times we would stop to swim and spear fish after a long day in the south. We usually took a lunch with us as the bad roads weren't conducive to going back and forth. One day "Greg" had gotten a couple of nice fish and was going after another. Becky saw a shark five or more feet long come right up on her daddy. She tired to get his attention, but he was intent on the fish that had gone into the rock where there could be moray eels. She screamed in the water and then went up to the surface and yelled "shark". When he heard her he flipped around and Becky said his flipper must have hit it in the nose because it sped off and her father just saw it going off. Beautiful water, but there were dangers.

There were other dangers on that island that you usually didn't think about. They were just a part of the terrain of a coral island with volcanic rock. Some of the sinkholes were big enough that they threw old cars in them to rust away. One natural phenomenon in Rock Sound is the

Ocean Hole. When the American Navy Base had been on Eleuthera some of the sailors were curious as to how far down it went. They finally put dye in the water and it came out almost to the states. The tide goes up and down with the tide there.

We became aware of how dangerous even the little sink holes could be. They were all around in the area of our house where Lance loved to play. While trying to get from one side to the other his foot slipped and he went down on the stump of a small tree that had been whacked off when they used that land for farming. It pierced his body and went up into his abdominal area eight inches. He came running to the house crying, "Daddy, I need you."

We rushed him to the doctor at Rock Sound and then to Princess Margaret Hospital in Nassau. They were unable to do anything for him. We called the American Embassy who contacted the American Coast Guard. All they wanted to know was if he was an American citizen. Although he had been born in Brazil he had dual citizenship because his parents were American. They sent a four engine plane for us with a medic aboard. An ambulance met us at the airport and we arrived at Jackson Memorial Hospital in Miami shortly after midnight. He was operated on soon afterwards. They cleaned leaves, broken pieces of wood and several units of blood from his intestinal region. He also had a temporary colostomy because of the danger of infection. He was at the hospital for three weeks and made good progress in spite of bleeding problems, incision infection, intestinal blockage, and the seriousness of the wound.

One of the "all things working together for good" that came out of that is that they discovered that Lance had a factor eight deficiency and not factor nine as he was diagnosed when he was one year old. Knowing this made a big difference in his future treatment.

While he recuperated—seeing doctors weekly—Sue and he remained in the states with Melody in Largo, Florida. She was getting settled in her new home and I helped her to get ready for her wedding to Ron Brown. "Greg" returned to the Bahamas to continue his work there. He returned for the wedding.

Because of Lance's hemophilia and his recent accident his doctors strongly suggested we live in the states with a good hospital and a doctor familiar with hemophilia. The Lord opened the door to this opportunity, with MAF (Missionary Aviation Fellowship) while we were in the states because of Lance's accident.

Hospitality Ministry

After Lance's accident in the Bahamas we moved to Miami to be closer to medical help. Harris went on loan from Gospel Missionary Union to Missionary Aviation Fellowship and worked for them as office manager. His pilot's license, engineering experience, and work in research and development with the U.S. Government prepared him well for the job. Susan completed a year's course as a medical technician and worked for a dermatologist, Dr. Peppercorn, which helped pay for the mortgage on our home.

Lance was at North Miami Beach High School and also volunteered at a local hospital. He was also in the North Miami Beach High School Marching Band and the Greater Miami String Band. Because of problems with his left knee he was taking his blood concentrate intravenously every other day for a year and a half and finally went to Harvard Medical Center in Boston for that problem. Over 150 people gave blood to help pay for his Factor 8 concentrate.

We saw the need for a place for missionaries to stay. Several places that were accommodating missionaries had recently closed down or accepted only their own missionaries. The MAF planes would often bring back those needing accommodations.

During the period from January, 1983 to September 5, 1983, we entertained 156 people. These were representative of 17 different countries. People came from or went to Ecuador, Bahamas, Bolivia,

Canada, St. Kitts, Bonaire, Honduras, Guatemala, U.S.A., Brazil, Belize, Venezuela, Colombia, Surinam, Costa Rica, Dominican Republic, and Haiti. These were in our prayer letter at that time.

They came from or representing the following missions: Gospel Missionary Union, World Relief, Campus Crusade, SAM, World Gospel Mission, Trans-World Radio, Child Evangelism, Baptist Mid-Missions, United World Mission, Helps International, TEAM, MBM, Canadian Church of God, New Tribes, and Teen Mission.

They were passing through Miami for various reasons. The majority were missionaries coming from or going to their field. They would often do their buying here as shipping was expensive from other parts of the states. Miami is a good place to get anything you need and Harris accumulated much experience to know where the best place was to buy things. Missionaries and Nationals came here for medical reasons. Some came for surgery and stayed for recuperation. We also hosted teams that were going to help out on mission fields. Young people who were returning to the fields for the summer were coming and going during that time. In the fall we accommodated those who were going to study in the states and couldn't make good flight connections. They came and stayed with us until they could get a flight out. Some stopped here to ship baggage, cars, and see embassies, just rest, or visit supporters. Whatever the reason, our home was their home away from home. I Peter 4:9-10 Be hospitable to one another without grumbling. As each one has received a gift, minister it to one another, as good stewards of the manifold grace of God.

Triumph out of Tragedy (His Title)

The following was an assignment written by Lance near the end of his senior year of high school.

In Brazil where I was born, we lived for years among Indians whose existence was dependent on their skill in making their bows and arrows and learning to hit the mark. They went to great pains to be sure the stick was straight and strong and that nothing was left on the shaft to divert it from its target. I have found constantly in my life how painful a misplaced arrow can be and how my life has to be re-aimed and new goals and plans substituted for the old.

Due to complications related to my hemophilia, we moved from Brazil to be nearer to proper medical help. The Bahamas seemed to be a good alternative. So many exciting things happened in this beautiful tropical setting: so many exciting and horrible things.

While living in the Bahamas, one day I was on an outing in a typical native garden. As I walked through the rocky garden, I attempted, for sport and excitement, to navigate a large and tree-filled hole. As I stepped from the edge, in an instant, my life was to change in such a drastic way. My foot slipped, and as I fell, I felt my body pierced by an old stump. Raising myself and feeling my wound, my hand was covered with blood. I did not panic, but with strong survival instinct, I ran to my house calling for my father.

Once we had arrived at Jackson Memorial Hospital in Miami, eleven hours after the accident, the doctors informed us that I had lost three fourths of my blood. I was bent with great pain. The surgery lasted for three hours and fifteen minutes. An incision was made the length of my stomach, through which my bowels were lifted out and laid on a table next to me for further inspection.

After my intestines were so neatly put aside, however, they were attached at both ends. At this point the doctors began the gruesome task of removing from my intestinal cavity sticks, leaves, and four units of blood.

After three weeks in the hospital, I finally was discharged feeling weak and thin. The doctors advised my parents that we should live in Miami from now on. Four months later we moved to North Miami Beach.

There was one glorious fact which emerged from this disaster. When I was a year old, I was diagnosed as a factor 9 hemophiliac. After the operation when I wouldn't stop bleeding the doctors found out that factor 9 was not missing in my blood, but that factor 8 was the actual factor I needed. Through this discovery, it has cut down drastically the pain of joint bleeds and the recovery time.

Another drastic change in my life occurred only a few months ago, in early February, 1986. This change was very subtle, not drastic as before. This time I began to notice certain changes in my intellectual abilities. After three visits to doctors proved unsuccessful, my condition only grew worse.

One morning I became so sick my parents quickly rushed me to the emergency room at Jackson Memorial Hospital. There at this much more advanced institution, the doctors quickly diagnosed my problem. After several tests, which showed reflexes, vision, hearing and strength, they determined that it was indeed a toxoplasmosis infection on the brain. By the time I had reached the hospital, my right side had lost its function causing my right arm and leg to be almost useless. After an emergency CAT scan, it was determined with accuracy and precision to what stage my condition had advanced. This scientific marvel showed in just a few minutes the extent and location of my lesion. It was found to be on the left hemisphere of my brain. A single large area of infection the size of a silver dollar could be seen clearly in my brain tissue surrounded by a large dark area of swelling.

The few days in the hospital, followed by a long period of recovery were painful and heartrending for me. Those days of recovery progressed agonizingly slow. I had no strength to turn over or move in bed. Horrible and abstract dreams as a result of my medicine also stole my rest. In one dream I had to read larger and more incomprehensible volumes of literature each evening. A massive library with countless volumes seemed to imprison me. Sometimes dark hooded figures seemed to walk away from me faceless in the gloom. They walked along a barren road. If there was plant life, it seemed to be scorched and as brown as the road.

Sitting and lying became an experience in pain. Any wrinkle or lump would grow until it became like a bed of rocks. I would shift constantly looking for any comfortable position. The pain was accompanied by a fever which wracked my body day and night. I would sit in my chair as still as possible, crying out to God for relief of such agony. The relief came when my fever broke, leaving my body soaked in sweat from my head to my waist.

Even now three months later, I still have dreams, reading and writing are occasionally difficult and my comprehension of calculus is still difficult. Earlier in the year I received a half scholarship from the University of Miami as well as a one thousand dollar National Merit Scholarship also provided by UM. I was also accepted into their Honors Medical Program.

A few weeks ago, however, my father noticed in the newspaper an article on the FIU/SECOM doctor of osteopathy program. Applying immediately, hope came into my heart. Now I have a full scholarship at FIU, spending money and a D.O. after seven years. And one of the best benefits is that I can live at home. These are wonderful plans for the next seven years that I hope don't get changed this time.

As always, joy and happiness were brought out of trials and tribulations. Through each one of my trials and periods of agony, I've always maintained a peace in my heart knowing that nothing could affect me that the Lord would not allow. I think back to the first instance when I was lying close to death, and I realize that there was a purpose in it all beyond human comprehension. When I recovered, I went about my life as normal as possible always keeping in my mind the perfect destiny that I have. With the toxoplasmosis infection, I experienced much peace in the midst of pain. I look again for the glorious purpose that will show itself. I believe that in weakness there is strength, and I am like gold tried in the fire and brought out purer.

The arrows which have been fired in my life have often turned awry, changing the aspirations, dreams, and hopes. But only the arrows fired by God can give you peace in sorrow and joy in agony.

We can never conceive just what life will hold. The future is obscure but definite. If we seek God's will for our lives, He will guide us through life one way or another but always with a peace that passes all understanding.

Lance's Home Going

August 26, 1986 – Miami Herald

Lance Victor Gregory, won merit scholarship

By Belinda Brockman, Herald Staff Writer

Lance Victor Gregory worked extra hard to reach his dream of becoming a country doctor. As a doctor, he could help the ailing, including those that suffered as he, from hemophilia.

Now, the dream is not possible.

Lance Gregory, a 1986 National Merit Scholarship winner, died Wednesday of an infection his body could not ally. He was 18.

"His body just grew too sick to handle it, with the low immune system," said Lance's father, G. Harris. "He couldn't fight it."

In February, Lance was diagnosed as having HTLV-III antibodies, the virus that caused AIDS, apparently acquired through a blood transfusion.

"He was truly an outstanding student. One of the most outstanding I've come across in a lot of years," said Bessie Gibson, principal of North Miami Beach High School, from which Lance graduated this past spring, "He was such a gentleman."

"A straight-A student," his dad boasted. "He had a lot of accomplishments.

A saxophonist in the concert band and a member of the math club. Lance attended summer school during his three years at North Miami Beach High School so that he could take extra math and science courses, his father said. All the better to prepare himself for his chosen career.

When he walked across the stage in his white cap and gown last spring to receive his diploma, Lance was in the top percent of his class. This fall, he would have attended Florida International University on a full scholarship.

But Lance also "got involved in things beyond the classroom," said Gibson. As part of a school project his senior year, he helped set up a free eye screening program at Southeastern Medical Center, contacting doctors personally to urge them to participate.

Lance enjoyed "fooling around with electronics," said his father. He built models and rockets and loved to snorkel and swim.

The son of missionaries, Lance was born in Brazil, where he lived eight years. But because his parents feared the possibility of not receiving proper medical care for his hemophilic condition, Lance and his family moved to the Bahamas.

Five years ago, after a life-threatening accident, they moved to Miami.

"He was very gentle and caring," said his father.

In addition to his father, survivors include his mother, Susan; two brothers, Christopher and Mark; two sisters, Melody Brown and Rebecca Mintz; and maternal grandparents, Lester and Mary Briggs.

Services will be at 8 p.m. Saturday at the Fred Hunter Hollywood Memorial Gardens home.

Love for a Very Special Child

A meeting was held quite far from earth.
It's time again for another birth,
said the angels to the Lord above.
This special child will need much love.
So let's be careful where he's sent.
We want his life to be content.
Please Lord find the parents who
Will do a special job for you.
They won't realize right away.
The leading role they're asked to play.
But with this child sent from above
Come stronger faith and richer love.
And soon they'll know the privilege given,
In caring for this human gift from heaven.
This precious child so meek and mild,
Is God's uniquely special child.

One of the chapters in the Bible, the 139 Psalm, that Lance learned included these thoughts, "You made all the delicate, inner parts of my body. You saw me before I was born and scheduled each day of my life before I began to breathe. Every day was recorded in your Book!" (TLB)

God planned Lance and his life and now he has ended his suffering by taking him home to glory. The void left in our lives can only be filled by Christ and the hope of being together with him again throughout eternity. He gave evidence of the hope that was within him to family, schoolmates and friends.

Our good friends Dr. and Mrs. Burton Goddard, who considered him "almost their boy," expressed their thoughts like this: "Never was a boy loved more, never was a boy given more tender loving care, never was there a finer boy, never was there a braver boy, never did a boy achieve more despite handicaps."

Psalm 71:1-8

El Paso Texas

In 1988, after the death of our son Lance from HIV/AIDS, we moved from humid Florida on the eastern sea coast to the dry desert mountains of the southwest. We traded the citrus and palm trees for cactus and tumbleweed. Once again great distances separated us from our families.

We did have a new family among the GMU missionaries – 21 in all. One of them, Willis Wantoch was our language teacher. We had another problem-changing our language from Portuguese to Spanish. After living in a house loaned to us for most of the first year we finally moved into our own home in a new neighborhood in eastern El Paso. Almost all of the neighbors were second generation Mexican/US citizens. Most of them had gone to UTEP (University of Texas at El Paso) and both of the parents had good paying jobs. They had brought legal and illegal relatives or friends from Mexico to help take care of their children and household needs.

At a birthday party for one of the children of our next door neighbor, we met Lourdes Oros. She had two children there, Holly and Sarah. Lourdes was the attractive wife of Marty Oros who worked for Roadway Moving Company as a representative to attract customers. As Harris talked with Lourdes he found out she was at UTEP and having trouble with her math – his specialty. While the children batted the piñata, he also discovered that she was a Christian. Marty was from a staunch catholic background. Lourdes hadn't attended church since they were married. When Harris shared with her that he was a missionary and would like to start a Bible Study in the neighborhood, she immediately said what every missionary wants to hear. "Oh, would you start a Bible Study with my husband and me?" We did, and after every Bible study she would turn to Marty and say, "Can we go to church now?" He would answer, "No, Lourdes. I'm not ready yet to go."

While she was at UTEP, her mother, Rosaberta, who lived with them, kept Holly and Sarah. She was there at the party too and while talking with me she asked if we could trade conversation in Spanish and English so that we both could improve our languages. So almost every day I would go down the street and talk with her. She also wanted to have a Spanish Bible Study and went around to all the homes in our area inviting the Spanish speaking to our Bible study. That was a big help as most of the help, especially the "illegals", won't answer the door. Some of them were caught and sent back to Mexico. Before they were, we tried to make sure they had a Bible and were taking Bible Correspondence courses.

Our neighbor's sister and her husband who lived in the lower valley were Christians. They had converted their garage into a chapel. They were sharing the gospel there with their friends and neighbors in Spanish. We got involved in helping them. The Lord had opened doors to all of these ministries through one birthday party invitation.

Lourdes and Marty were the key the Lord used to help us. Marty was interested at first and very friendly but reluctant to leave his catholic inheritance and life style. After he finally accepted the Lord he not only got very involved in helping us but also active at Grace Chapel. They invited relatives, friends, neighbors, colleagues from UTEP, customers and business associates of Marty's to our Bible study. When he was transferred to Douglas, Arizona, it gave us an outreach to that area.

They became active in a church in Double Adobe and later a Baptist church in Tucson, AR.

Neighborhood Watch with its meetings and parties gave us close connections with all of our neighbors. One Halloween, instead of handing out candies as before, we cooperated in serving plates of rice, beans, yucca and beefies to Mexicans and El Pasoans trick or treating. Crime in all of El Paso was high and the Neighborhood Watch was very important. It saved several in our neighborhood from being robbed. Most houses have steel bars on their doors and windows. We and others had signs in our front windows and any child who felt threatened could come to our house and we would help them.

Harris was also very involved with the GMU churches in Juarez and Zaragosa, Mexico in construction. He worked with the other missionary men and used his expertise as an engineer and builder. They also had several groups that came from churches, schools, medical groups, and *Helps International Mission* to help with the construction.

In 1996 Mark, Janet and Melody's family came to El Paso and we all took a trip to the Grand Canyon, Petrified Forest and Painted Desert. Susan helped Heather and Heath earn their Junior Ranger Badges helping to clean up those areas.

Our last summer there Mark's three oldest children, Dan, Joshua, and Tabitha were with us and the boys helped with the construction in Mexico. They also attended the camp at Glenwood New Mexico.

We were active with a church, Grace Chapel, who supported us in our work. Through them we helped at the camp in Glenwood, near the Arizona border in the beautiful Gila Mountains. Harris was on the Board of the camp. We enjoyed working with the young people there in the summer camps and also with retreats and conferences during the off season.

After turning 65 in 1993 Harris was manager of the Shepherd Retirement Community in Frostproof, Florida. I worked in the office as his secretary and was in charge of ten rental homes to seasonal visitors. In 1998 we moved to Moore Haven, Florida. We were active in the First Baptist Church there and also ministered in the Grace Nursing Home in Clewiston, Florida. We also held early Sunday morning services at the Moore Haven Yacht Club. The directors of the Club furnished us with coffee and home made goodies so that we could visit with the residents and travelers after the meeting.

In 2006 Harris died from complications of a fall. Shortly after that Susan moved to Bradenton Missionary Village (now renamed II Villaggio) where she is now living.

Brazil Work Today – 2010

How different the work is for missionaries in Brazil today. Reservations have been established and no missionaries or Brazilians can live on Indian land. The seed that has been sown by missionaries and Indian leaders has brought forth fruit and a desire among the Indians themselves to go and share. Some Terena Indians from the SAM Bible Institute have gone into other tribes and continued the work or started it. South America Mission is focusing on leadership development to prepare the Indians themselves from each tribe to reshape their communities for generations to come with the love of Jesus. To do this a practical Bible Institute, Ammi Training Center was established. They bring leaders from each tribe and teach them how to get along with former enemies. They start with primitive cultures and teach them to read and write in Portuguese. Of course the missionary bases all these things on Bible teaching and the development of spiritual disciplines.

Needless to say it is not easy to transport these groups from their primitive world to the modern way of life. It takes much prayer, dependence on the Holy Spirit, and funds. To us who concentrated on one tribe at a time, it seems an overwhelming task. But the Lord is over and above any human efforts.

The students from the school are taken twice a year to other tribes to do "missionary work" and get a taste of the joy of seeing others reached for Christ. Over 200 students representing 36 different tribal groups have studied the Word of God at Ammi. The majority of the 73 graduates are serving the Lord.

In the 1990's and early this century, a group of Indians, including some of the AMMI teachers and students, formed a group called Complei to unite the different indigenous people in the Amazon basin. They are going themselves to more effectively fulfill God's great commandment to reach the remaining tribes that have never heard the story of God sending His son Jesus to die in their place.

In 2012, July 4 – 8, SAM and the Ammi Training Center will host Complei 2012. In 2008, 1600 attended with 49 different tribes represented from seven different countries.

This Complei Congress is expected to bring together 3000 or more pastors and lay leaders. More than 60 ethnic groups will be represented as well as leaders of those working among the indigenous population. Plans are being formulated for expanding temporary meeting and dining space, dorm and bathing facilities and bringing water from neighboring sources. It's a gigantic undertaking that needs much prayer.

God's plan is being carried out. It doesn't depend on one family or one tribe. His plan is for all to hear. It's our duty to go, give and pray.

End

CPSIA information can be obtained at www.ICGtesting.com
Printed in the USA
238803LV00004B/3/P

9 781426 956775